UNCHARTED

UNCHARTED

How Trump Beat Biden, Harris,
and the Odds in the Wildest
Campaign in History

CHRIS WHIPPLE

HARPER
INFLUENCE

An Imprint of HarperCollins*Publishers*

HarperCollins books may be purchased for educational, business, or sales promotional use. For information, please email the Special Markets Department at SPsales@harpercollins.com.

FIRST EDITION

Library of Congress Cataloging-in-Publication Data has been applied for.

ISBN 978-0-063386211

25 26 27 28 29 LBC 5 4 3 2 1

This one is for Sam.

CONTENTS

"WHAT THE FUCK HAPPENED TO THIS GUY?"

Joe Biden looked like a dead man walking. From the moment he'd arrived at Camp David, the rustic presidential retreat in Maryland's Catoctin Mountain Park, Ron Klain, head of Biden's debate prep team, had been shocked by his condition. It was Sunday, June 23, 2024, four days before Biden's make-or-break debate with Donald Trump on CNN. Sitting with him in Aspen Lodge, the presidential cabin, Klain was struck by how exhausted he was—and how out of touch with his own campaign.

"He didn't know what Trump had been saying and couldn't grasp what the back and forth was," Klain recalled. The president abruptly announced that he needed to get some sun. He shuffled out the door and off to the pool, where he sank into a lounge chair and fell sound asleep.

Later that evening, Klain coaxed Biden back to Aspen Lodge, where he gave him a stack of 3x5 cards with messages about his economic agenda. It was important, Klain told the president, to outline his plans for a second term. Biden, irritated, pushed back.

He didn't care about that; he wanted to talk about how much foreign leaders loved him.

Lately Biden had been obsessed with the opinion of foreign leaders. The president was especially fixated on French president Emmanuel Macron and German chancellor Olaf Scholz. "Well," he told Klain, "these guys say I'm doing a great job as president so I must be a great president."

The president was fatigued, befuddled, and disengaged. Klain feared the debate with Trump could be a nationally televised disaster.

At the age of 81, Joe Biden was running for reelection. Overwhelmingly, Americans opposed the idea. For months he'd been subjected to a growing clamor within the Democratic Party urging him to pass the torch to a younger candidate. In interviews on cable television, James Carville, the "Ragin' Cajun" who'd led Bill Clinton's campaign to victory in 1992, had been calling for Biden to step aside. David Axelrod, the rumpled chief strategist of Barack Obama's winning 2008 campaign, had echoed Carville's admonition: The stakes were too high in 2024 to risk everything on a candidate who was well beyond his prime.

You didn't have to be a famous presidential campaign strategist to know that Biden's reelection was in serious jeopardy. According to an Associated Press-NORC poll taken in August 2023, 77 percent of Americans, and 69 percent of Democrats, were against Biden running for a second term. The argument for Biden's abdication wasn't just political, it was actuarial. Anyone who'd ever had to persuade an octogenarian grandfather to give up the car keys knew that Biden was just too old to serve another four years as president.

But Joe Biden was having none of it. And neither was his inner circle of family, friends, and advisers. Despite months of public opinion polling that showed Biden losing to Trump in the critical battleground states, they were all-in on his bid for reelection. Their reasons were both understandable and troubling.

On the one hand, Biden's true believers had reason to doubt the naysayers. They'd been wrong before. During the 2020 Democratic presidential primary, the experts had pronounced Biden politically dead after he placed fourth in the Iowa Caucus and fifth in the New Hampshire primary. But after stunning victories in the South Carolina and Super Tuesday primaries, he'd gobsmacked his critics by winning the nomination and beating Trump in the general election by seven million votes. In 2024, Biden's friends and close aides believed, the doubters were wrong again.

Moreover, it was an article of faith in Biden World that the big Democratic donors were against him. "I remember going to a conference of rich people at Aspen in 2023," said Klain. "They were all like, 'He needs to get out. We're tired of him.' He pissed off a lot of people who were the powers in our party." Why should Biden listen to a bunch of plutocrats over the working-class Democrats who'd put him in the Oval Office?

Biden's allies also believed that the media were out to get him. That was understandable given the blatant pro-MAGA bias of right-wing mouthpieces like FOX News and Breitbart. But in their view *The New York Times* was the worst offender; the newspaper of record had relentlessly pounded the president over his age while barely reporting his extraordinary achievements: an economy rescued from free fall; a once-in-a-century pandemic alleviated; major bipartisan legislation passed by a 50–50 Congress; the West rallied against Putin's invasion of a democracy in the heart of Europe. If Biden's polls were bad, his inner circle believed, it was because the mainstream press had turned a blind eye to his record of historic accomplishments.

And yet none of this changed the fact that Joe Biden had aged dramatically while in office. His physical frailty was obvious—the hobbled gait when he boarded Air Force One and the way he shuffled stiffly to a lectern. Equally apparent was his verbal impairment—struggling to complete his thoughts; transposing the names of Harris and Trump and confusing the presidents of Egypt and Mexico. But Biden's cognitive impairment was more serious than that.

Many people who saw the president in private said he was mentally diminished. There were days when he fired on almost every cylinder, commanding the nuances of Middle East diplomacy. But he often lost the thread of a conversation or repeated anecdotes he'd told a few minutes ago. A veteran Democratic operative who interviewed with Biden and his aides for a top campaign job believed the president "didn't know what was going on" and that his advisers were covering it up. The job interview was unintentionally revealing: While the COVID crisis had enabled them to keep the president in his basement during the 2020 campaign, they told her, "We no longer have that excuse. What do we do?" Friends who spoke with Biden at fundraisers couldn't believe how much he'd aged. Even at small gatherings in donors' living rooms where presidents are almost always unscripted, Biden spoke from teleprompters.

The truth was that Joe Biden was too old to run for reelection, much less govern effectively in a second term. His advisers knew this, or should have known it, but refused to face that fact. None ever discussed with the president whether he was too old to serve a second term. Instead, they walled Biden off from the outside world, limiting the number of people who interacted with him. Senators complained they rarely saw the president. One prominent Democrat, an old friend of Biden's, told me he'd visited the White House twelve times but no one had ever suggested that he pop into the Oval Office to say hello. The reason for this seemed obvious to him: The president wasn't up to it.

I had my own reasons for wondering if Joe Biden's White House staff had been hiding him. When, in September of 2022, I asked for an interview with Biden for my book on the first two years of his White House, *The Fight of His Life*, it was granted on one condition: I would send my questions by email and Biden would answer them in writing. It seemed clear that the president's aides didn't want to risk having him interact in real time with a reporter.

This book is the story of how Washington, D.C.'s powers-that-be dealt with an incumbent president, hobbled by old age, who refused to give up his bid for reelection. It's also the story of how he ultimately relented, turning the most consequential election in modern U.S. history upside down. Biden's eleventh-hour decision to step away from the ticket was undoubtedly the correct one. But did his delay in passing the torch to a successor cost Democrats the election against Donald Trump? This book will explore that question.

BY THE TIME BIDEN ARRIVED AT CAMP DAVID TO PREPARE FOR his debate with Trump, he was more isolated than ever. At this point in his presidency, Biden's entourage consisted of just five people: Mike Donilon, his message guru; Steve Ricchetti, his legislative affairs expert; Bruce Reed, his domestic policy adviser; Anthony Bernal, the first lady's chief of staff and the president's "body man"; and Annie Tomasini, his deputy chief of staff.

Klain, Biden's former White House chief of staff, was one of his staunchest loyalists. He'd prepared eight previous presidential candidates for televised debates, but the stakes had never been this high; Biden's performance against Trump could decide the 2024 election, one of the most consequential in U.S. history. A poor outing would clinch the widespread perception that Biden was too infirm to be president.

When he awoke at Camp David on Tuesday morning, June 25—two days before the debate—the president's voice was shot. He took two COVID tests, which came back negative. Klain and his team decided to attempt a mock debate. Bob Bauer, the president's personal lawyer and husband of Biden aide Anita Dunn, played the role of Trump. Dunn played a CNN moderator. It didn't go well for Biden. "He didn't really understand what his argument was on inflation," said Klain. "He didn't really understand what his proposals had been. And he had nothing to say about a second term other than to finish the job."

Was there any way to cancel the CNN debate? The answer was no. Given the controversy over the president's age and cognitive condition, not showing up wasn't a politically viable option.

The next day, Biden, who still felt ill, had an idea. If he looked perplexed when Trump talked, voters would understand that Trump was an idiot. Klain replied: "Sir, when you look perplexed, people just think you're perplexed. And this is our problem in this race."

On the morning of the debate, June 27, Biden felt slightly better. The president departed on Marine One, the presidential helicopter, for Maryland's Joint Base Andrews, where Air Force One was waiting to fly him to Atlanta.

Biden's motorcade arrived at CNN minutes before the debate began. "There was no reason to be early because he was president of the United States," said Klain. "They weren't going to start without him." Biden was introduced by the CNN anchors and stepped onto the stage. On live television, before an estimated 51 million viewers, the president approached his lectern. His complexion was ghostly white—like a cadaver that had been prepared for an open-casket Irish wake.

Biden muddled through the first ten minutes, his voice so soft it was almost a whisper. When Trump spoke, the president looked befuddled. Then, at the twelve-minute mark, came the moment Biden's supporters had been dreading.

Asked about the national debt, the president said that he was "making sure that we're able to make every single solitary person eligible for what I've been able to do with the COVID—excuse me, dealing with everything we have to do with . . ."

Biden stopped. He looked lost.

Then he stammered, "Uh, look, if . . . we finally beat Medicare." He stared into the camera.

Klain swallowed hard. "This is a disaster," he thought. Biden had just stopped, midsentence, inexplicably frozen. Klain couldn't help but think "This is going to feed the narrative, not solve our narrative."

The ordeal would continue for another two hours and six minutes; in the end, Biden couldn't complete his two-minute closing summation. Afterward, on a small stage at an Atlanta hotel, as demoralized supporters looked on, Jill Biden assured her husband that nothing was wrong. "You did such a great job. You answered every question!" she gushed. "You knew all the facts!" But something was terribly wrong.

One of Biden's closest friends had watched the debate from his apartment in New York City. Though he knew the president wasn't as sharp as he used to be, he'd never seen him like this. At

12:30 a.m., as he was about to turn in, suddenly his phone lit up. It was the president's sister, Val. She was weeping and enraged.

"What did they *do* to my brother at Camp David?" she shouted. Valerie Biden Owens knew something about political debates. Until stepping aside in 2020, she'd managed Joe Biden's campaigns since 1972, when, as a precocious 29-year-old neophyte, he'd toppled the venerable Republican Caleb Boggs, in a stunning upset, to win a Senate seat from Delaware. Val was a ruthless campaigner and her brother's fiercest defender.

On the other end of the call, Joe's friend tried to console her, but she was so angry, she was practically incoherent. The phone went silent. She'd hung up.

The next morning his phone lit up again. It was Val. She was still furious but more composed—and looking for someone to blame. "How could he get there just ten minutes before the debate?" she snapped. "How could he have no walk-through? How could he not be told the camera angles? How could the makeup person, whoever the makeup person was, make him up like that? He had a good tan. He looked good. How could they make him up to look like Dorian Gray? How did *that* happen?"

Joe's friend had no answers.

A few days later, his phone buzzed again. The familiar baritone voice, much stronger than it had been during the debate, was unmistakable. "It's Joe," he said. There was a pause. "Joe Biden."

His friend replied: "Yeah, *no shit*."

Biden burst out laughing. "Hey, thanks for talking Valerie off the ledge," the president said.

"No problem," his friend replied. "You don't have to thank me."

Biden paused and then said, "What do you think?"

Biden's friend couldn't resist this softball over the plate. "About what?" he said.

Biden cracked up again. The president laughed for four or five seconds. And then, "in a very strong voice filled with timbre," as his friend recalled, "he said, 'Hey man, that's why I love you. You're a fucking *wise* guy.' And as he said it, I thought to myself, 'Where did *that* voice go? Where did *that* guy with that voice go? What the fuck happened to this guy?'"

It was the question on which the political fate of the nation would turn. What had happened to that guy during the debate? And what did it mean for Biden's candidacy? Was the president's shocking incoherence just an aberration, a "bad night," as his handlers were insisting?

Was he ill-prepared by his debate prep team, as his sister, Valerie, seemed to believe? Or did he have some kind of chronic mental impairment?

If Biden were just suffering from fatigue or a bad cold, then maybe he could recover and defeat Trump. But if he was *non compos mentis*, incapable of making the case against the former president, then the Democratic ticket was headed toward a cliff.

How had the country ended up here? Had the president's advisers engaged in wishful thinking about his ability to overcome the effects of aging? Or did they cover up his condition in order to stay in power?

The Democratic Party, and the country, were caught in a terrible quandary. First, no one except Biden, his family, and his doctors knew the truth about his condition. And second, even if Biden *were* mentally impaired, only he could decide to forego his reelection bid. Fourteen million Americans had voted for Biden in the primaries, giving him 3,904 delegates (1,975 were needed for the nomination). Only Biden could surrender those delegates by stepping aside.

And in that event, the nomination might be contested by a number of ambitious Democratic aspirants—not only Vice President Kamala Harris, but governors such as California's Gavin Newsom, Michigan's Gretchen Whitmer, and Illinois's JB Pritzker.

Harris, who for two years had struggled to find her footing as Biden's vice president, had grown into the job; she'd gained confidence in the national security arena and found her voice as a defender of women's reproductive rights. But few people thought that in the span of a few weeks she could unite the party and lead a winning campaign against a vicious political street brawler like Donald Trump. Time was short. The Democratic National Convention was scheduled to kick off in Chicago on August 19.

Whoever became the Democratic nominee would face an emboldened Trump, who would emerge from the GOP convention in Milwaukee full of confidence and bravado. There was a reason Joe Biden was determined to keep running. He didn't think Kamala Harris or anyone else could beat Trump.

The country's fate was in Biden's hands. But what happened next would also be shaped by the people who had his ear: family members, close friends, and loyal aides to whom Biden had turned for advice during times of crisis over decades. Some other powerful figures would play key roles. They were trusted allies who Biden would come to believe abandoned him: Nancy Pelosi, Chuck Schumer, Hakeem Jeffries, and George Clooney.

After the debate, the Biden White House was less like the TV series *The West Wing* and more like *House of Cards*. Or, as Biden's aide Anita Dunn tartly observed in a farewell toast with staffers, Francis Ford Coppola's film *The Godfather*.

Before his televised implosion, Biden's aides, friends, and family were remarkably united. But in the aftermath of the debate, the long knives came out. The president believed that his friend and ally Nancy Pelosi had betrayed him. Klain blamed the party's elites and rich donors for forcing Biden out. Dunn blamed the elites and the press. The president's sister, Valerie, blamed her brother's debate prep team. And almost everyone, including Biden, blamed Barack Obama.

Some of Biden's closest advisers locked horns. Ron Klain, waging a last-ditch campaign to keep Biden on the ticket, tangled with his successor as White House chief of staff, Jeff Zients. Retaining the nomination "would have been a bloody battle," Klain said. But surrendering it was worse—because then "the blood was on everyone." Joe Biden chose to give up that battle. At the end, miserable and suffering from COVID, isolated at his beach house and feeling abandoned, the president was alone.

This is the story of how a president reluctantly surrendered his nomination for the good of his party and the nation. It's a story with Shakespearean twists and turns, acts of treachery and betrayal, courage and grace.

This is also the story of how Kamala Harris, whose campaign for president in 2020 had ended in acrimony and embarrassment, rallied Democrats almost seamlessly around her unexpected candidacy in the summer of 2024. But the smooth handoff in public belied the turmoil that churned below the surface of her candidacy. A campaign that had been built to reelect Joe Biden never fully became her own.

Finally, it's the story of a man who tried to overturn a free and fair election, who was convicted of thirty-four felonies and found to have committed sexual abuse—it's the story of how that man convinced millions of Americans that he could fix their problems, and pulled off the greatest comeback in American political history.

Joe Biden's place in history would depend on what happened next. If Kamala Harris defeated Donald Trump, Biden would be celebrated for his courageous decision to step aside and endorse her. But if she lost, he would be judged harshly for not having abdicated much earlier, allowing a stronger candidate to emerge from a competitive primary. As early as the summer of 2024, some Democratic insiders believed that Biden's belated withdrawal would end badly. "If Harris loses," one of them told me in August, "the story is going to be the selfishness of Biden because he really fucked it up by staying in this thing. Because if she loses, why did it fuck up? Because it was too late in the game to introduce a pretty unknown person to pull this off."

As it turned out, Biden's last-minute passing of the baton to Kamala Harris ended in a devastating defeat for the first Black female nominee of a major party. But her candidacy, and her defeat, were not inevitable. Nor was the election of Donald Trump preordained.

The losers, Harris and her campaign staff, would have much to answer for. Months after the election, the finger-pointing and second guessing among Democrats would rage on. Biden's true believers argued that he never should have stepped aside. And Trump's campaign manager, Susie Wiles, offered a scathing postmortem on Kamala Harris and the race she ran, saying in an interview with me: "we couldn't believe how bad she was."

But to understand just how the 2024 presidential campaign came to be, and how it ultimately unfolded, we must go back to the spring of 2016. That's how the story begins, when Donald Trump believed he was being cheated—long before a single presidential vote had been cast.

1

"I SAW THE DAGGERS COMING OUT OF HIS EYES."

Paul Manafort was in a hurry. It was March 2016, and the veteran GOP political operative had been invited to dinner by Donald Trump at his gilded Palm Beach estate. Though he had a home in Palm Beach Gardens, Manafort, 67, didn't know the real estate tycoon–turned-would-be-president all that well. They'd met back in the 1980s, when Roger Stone, Manafort's pal and notorious GOP dirty trickster, had introduced them. Now Trump's dream of becoming president, formed almost four decades earlier, was no longer an impossibility.

Manafort was waved through the oceanfront gate by the security guard and walked into the lobby. The first person he saw was a scrawny figure with a crewcut and beady eyes. It was Corey Lewandowski, Trump's 42-year-old campaign manager. Manafort and Lewandowski stared at each other. "I saw the daggers coming out of Lewandowski's eyes," Manafort told me. "And that moment was the high point of our relationship. It only got worse from there."

Trump, Manafort, Lewandowski, and a few others had dinner not on the porch, where the billionaire usually held court with his wealthy club members, but in a private dining room. Lewandowski fumed like a jilted lover. According to David Bossie, one of Trump's aides in the room that evening, Trump's first words to Manafort were the same as when he first met Corey: "Wow, you're a good-looking guy."

Bossie, a Lewandowski ally who also coveted Trump's attention, couldn't help observing that Manafort, about thirty years older than Corey, "had had some work done to secure his youthful appearance."

When a reporter called him a few days later to ask about the Mar-a-Lago dinner, Lewandowski "knew from that moment on that Manafort was a leaker . . . [and that] Paul was a bad guy."

Actually, Lewandowski didn't know the half of it. Among the rogues' gallery of lobbyists and influence peddlers stretching back to the early 1980s, Manafort was *sui generis*, the biggest rogue of all. He was not only on speed dial with oligarchs and despots of the world's most corrupt regimes, but he was also up to his eyeballs in questionable deals, stashing lavish fees in offshore bank accounts.

Manafort's sketchy income from overseas clients had financed an almost cartoonishly opulent lifestyle. It kept him not only in Botox but in silk rugs, cashmere suits, garish antiques, and ostrich-leather bomber jackets. He had a fleet of Range Rovers and Mercedes, and luxurious homes from Alexandria, Virginia, to Palm Beach, Florida, to the Hamptons on Long Island. The annual gardening bill for his Hamptons estate—with a pool house, putting green, home theater, and tennis court—was $100,000.

And this didn't even count the strange tale of a suitcase allegedly stuffed with millions of dollars in cash from a foreign dictator. Cash that went mysteriously missing. But that's getting ahead of our story.

IN THE SPRING OF 2016, AS MANAFORT ENTERED HIS ORBIT, Donald Trump was a political force of nature. The writer Joe Klein had famously called Bill Clinton "the natural." But with his feral grasp of political campaigning and his instinct for the jugular, Trump, a first-time presidential candidate at 70, was, in his own way, every bit Clinton's equal. Preaching a potent brew of populist nativism, resentment, and conspiracy theories, Trump had rolled up victories in the GOP primaries.

In an era of income inequality and vanishing middle-class jobs, Trump understood the raw appeal of his assault on the country's elites. What he didn't understand was the arcana of the GOP electoral process. Trump didn't know how to translate winning primaries into accumulating delegates and gaining the nomination.

The whole thing was baffling. For example, Trump had romped in the GOP's Louisiana primary, capturing a majority of the vote. But a week later, most of the delegates were awarded to Texas senator Ted Cruz. Trump was furious. As Kellyanne Conway, his senior adviser, put it: "Remember, this is Donald Trump. If you sign a deal for *The Apprentice*, Oprah Winfrey doesn't become the host." Trump called Republican National Committee (RNC) chair Reince Priebus. "You guys are stealing my victories!" he barked.

Priebus, a dutiful, finger-in-the-wind GOP official from Wisconsin, had written the famous "postmortem" of his party after Mitt Romney's blow-out loss to Democrat Barack Obama in 2012. The road back to winning elections, his report concluded, was to build a larger, more inclusive GOP tent, one that would attract Latinos and voters of color. Priebus thought Trump, who'd railed about Mexican rapists and murderers, was a kind of bomb thrower who could blow up his party. But he was a bomb thrower with a real chance of winning the nomination. Priebus suggested they meet.

Trump and Lewandowski went to see Priebus at his office. The RNC head listened as Trump railed about stolen delegates. Priebus finally spoke up. "Donald, you don't know the rules, do you?" he said. "What do you mean?" Trump snapped. Priebus started to explain the eye-glazing details governing caucuses and primaries in various states. Trump looked at Lewandowski. "Did you know any of this?"

Lewandowski did not. At that moment, Trump's campaign manager might as well have been a Bond villain's lackey sitting on a trapdoor.

Trump started calling friends, asking them if they knew anyone who understood this stuff. Roger Stone and Thomas Barrack, CEO of the investment firm Colony Capital, told him that if he wanted someone who knew about delegates, Manafort was his man. In fact, Manafort *was* an expert on GOP primaries. Back in 1976, as a conservative, 27-year-old member of the Connecticut Young Republicans, Manafort worked for James A. Baker III, then Gerald Ford's chief delegate counter, wrangling delegates from Ford's rival Ronald Reagan. Manafort had been working on campaigns and running conventions ever since. When it came to counting delegates, he was a pro.

So began the process that brought Manafort to Mar-a-Lago for dinner. It also signaled Lewandowski's demise. Trump's former body man–turned–campaign manager was already on thin ice; he'd been arrested for battery after manhandling a female reporter. (Lewandowski wasn't prosecuted.) But more important, Trump needed someone who could navigate the political minefield ahead. "He was able to get a campaign from zero to frontrunner purely on his own skills," said Manafort of Trump. "But he needed somebody to come in behind him at that point and start building the architecture that would be necessary to manage his success. And that's what I was able to get him to understand: 'You're still going to be the reason we win. I'm simply going to be giving you the tools you need to have your victory matter.'"

Manafort joined the campaign as an unpaid adviser. Maybe he didn't need the money—or maybe he got something more valuable: a bargaining chip he could use with a shadowy figure to whom he allegedly owed money, Ukrainian oligarch Oleg Deripaska. Upon getting the job, Manafort reached out by email to an associate of Deripaska, asking if his new gig had been noticed: "How do we use it to get whole? Has OVD operation [Oleg Vladimirovich Deripaska] seen?"

For Trump, Lewandowski was a perfect fall guy. The boss needed someone to blame: Not only had he been screwed out of those Louisiana delegates, he'd been beaten by Cruz in the Wisconsin primary. Lewandowski knew the axe was about to fall. As he later wrote, Manafort was telling Trump that "it's all Corey's fault, he said. I thought Manafort was the cavalry coming to help. I didn't think he was coming to stick a shiv in my back—but that's what dishonest people do."

It fell to Trump's son Don Jr. and his fixer Michael Cohen to fire him. On June 20, 2016, they met with Lewandowski and did just that. Manafort sent out an email pronouncing himself campaign chairman.

Trump delighted in taunting Manafort. One day when he

was having lunch at his golf club in Bedminster, New Jersey—with his political strategist Steve Bannon, FOX News president Roger Ailes, and his sidekick Rudy Giuliani—Manafort, who hadn't been invited, found out about the lunch and drove down from the Hamptons to crash it.

Bannon never forgot Manafort's entrance. Dressed in a blue blazer with a crest on the breast pocket, he looked as if he'd just stepped off a yacht. "Thurston Howell III," thought Bannon. Furious over a recent piece in the *Times* in which Manafort claimed to manage him, Trump dressed him down. "Am I a baby, Paul?" Trump demanded. "Is that what you are saying, I'm a baby? You're terrible on TV. You've got no energy. You don't represent the campaign. I've told you nicely."

Unless your name was Jared or Ivanka Kushner, it was the kind of humiliation that sometimes came with working for Trump. In fact, Trump would subject Giuliani to an almost identical tirade when the former New York City mayor went on the Sunday talk shows and tried—lamely, in Trump's opinion—to explain away his disastrous *Access Hollywood* videotape.

Trump treated female staffers with more courtesy—in part because they didn't pretend to be his peers. At the Trump Organization, a company full of testosterone, the women just seemed to intuit this and use it to their advantage. Kellyanne Conway, a savvy, extroverted adviser who'd once worked for Ted Cruz, understood this rule but wasn't afraid to assert herself. Trump excoriated her one day when he dropped in unexpectedly on one of her campaign commercial shoots. "Am I paying for these people?" he complained, pointing to the actors. "Tell these people I'm not paying for them." But Conway wasn't intimidated. And Trump would eventually ask her to manage his campaign.

Although Manafort was now the campaign's chairman, the

person in charge of running it was a colorful Texan named Brad Parscale. A favorite of Kushner, Parscale had parlayed designing the Trump Organization website into a job as the campaign's digital director. But his responsibilities had grown to include not just social media but television advertising, fundraising, and turning out the vote. Parscale mined voters' Facebook data in innovative ways. He also worked with a firm, Cambridge Analytica, that tapped into private Facebook accounts. (The FTC later found that Cambridge Analytica had deceptively harvested personal information from tens of thousands of Facebook users.)

The 2016 Republican National Convention, which took place in Cleveland, Ohio, in July, was hardly a coronation; it featured Ted Cruz leading a raucous mutiny, calling on delegates to "vote your conscience." But for Trump, and for Manafort, it was a triumph. They'd crushed twenty rivals for the GOP nomination and revolutionized American politics with his scorched-earth behavior. As Kushner would later write: "Manafort executed a highly successful convention that was authentic to Trump and ensured that he secured delegates for the nomination."

But trouble was brewing. Rumors had been swirling about Manafort's shady dealings with a corrupt, Kremlin-backed party in Ukraine. On August 14, Manafort asked Steve Bannon, the slovenly alt-right firebrand and Trump adviser, to meet him at his apartment in Trump Tower. It was a beautiful place; Bannon was surprised to learn that Manafort owned it. When he arrived, his host looked anxious. Manafort showed Bannon the transcript of a *New York Times* story that had been sent to him for comment before publication. David Bossie described the scene in his memoir, written with Lewandowski, *Let Trump Be Trump*. The "woman in the muu-muu" was reportedly Manafort's wife, Kathy.

"Twelve-point-seven-million-dollar payment from Ukraine?"
asked Bannon.

The woman in the muu-muu sat bolt upright. "Paul?"
she said.

"How much of this is true?" Bannon asked.

"It's all lies," Manafort said. "My lawyers are fighting it."

The muu-muu–clad woman was now on her feet, her
arms folded.

"Paul, twelve million?"

"It was a long time ago," he said to her. "I had expenses."

The next morning, the *New York Times* broke the story
in its print edition, headlined "Secret Ledger in Ukraine Lists
Cash for Trump's Campaign Chief." The report alleged that
Manafort was involved in a corrupt network that was "used to
loot Ukrainian assets and influence elections during the administration of Mr. Manafort's main client, former President Viktor F.
Yanukovych." It continued:

Handwritten ledgers show $12.7 million in undisclosed
cash payments designated for Mr. Manafort from Mr. Yanu-
kovych's pro-Russian political party from 2007 to 2012 . . .
Investigators assert that the disbursements were part of an
illegal, off-the-books system whose recipients also included
election officials.

With allegations flying for months about the Trump campaign's alleged collusion with Russia, the *Times* report landed
like a bombshell in Trump World. It didn't help when reports
emerged that Manafort had met with an alleged Russian spy and
showed him internal Trump campaign polling data.

The whole thing was an unwelcome distraction and Trump had grown tired of it. He also missed the anything goes, "hunger and swagger" of the campaign's early days under Lewandowski. Trump dispatched Kushner to fire Manafort. (The boss hated firing anyone, despite the premise of his reality show.) Over breakfast at Cipriani, an opulent midtown Manhattan eatery, Kushner told Manafort it was time to go.

But Manafort would continue to advise the campaign privately. And the drama surrounding his dealings with dictators and oligarchs had only just begun.

Trump now named Steve Bannon and Kellyanne Conway as his chairman and campaign manager, respectively. Bannon, 62, who looked as though he always slept in his clothes, was hardly Trump's idea of a chairman from central casting. But Bannon's torch-and-pitchfork mentality amused him. Conway, 49, was one of the few people who held their own, sparring verbally with Trump. He didn't always follow her advice but enjoyed her give-and-take on messaging and strategy.

ON OCTOBER 7, 2016, NEWS BROKE OF A SCANDAL THAT WOULD have ended the presidential hopes of any normal candidate. In a previously unaired videotape from the TV program *Access Hollywood*, Trump was captured bantering with a correspondent named Billy Bush. Trump matter-of-factly declared that he grabbed women by their private parts without their consent—because "when you're a star, they let you do it. You can do anything."

The resulting uproar sent GOP party officials scrambling for cover. This was a bridge too far for some party officials. House Speaker Paul Ryan canceled an event in Wisconsin where he was scheduled to appear with Trump. GOP senators condemned his outrageous comments. Was it too much to hope that the party's leaders might come together and, for the sake of decency and the party's future, find a way to replace Trump as the nominee? Yes, it was.

The *Access Hollywood* flap had the unexpected effect of injecting discipline into Donald Trump. For the rest of the campaign he was on his best behavior, refraining from tweeting or daring the Russians to steal emails or bragging about sexual assault. Meanwhile, inadvertently or not, FBI Director James Comey was hatching an October Surprise: reopening an investigation into Hillary Clinton's handling of classified emails.

The country was on the verge of the most shocking upset in American presidential history.

And yet unbeknownst to voters was another Trump scandal that would remain hidden for almost eight years. As *The Washington Post* would report in 2024, five days before Trump took office in 2017, an Egyptian bank official was asked to "kindly withdraw" nearly $10 million—all in cash. *The Post* continued:

> *Inside the state-run National Bank of Egypt, employees were soon busy placing bundles of $100 bills into two large bags, according to records from the bank. Four men arrived and carried away the bags . . . classified U.S. intelligence [indicated] that Egyptian President Abdel Fatah El-Sisi sought to give Trump $10 million to boost his 2016 presidential campaign, a* Washington Post *investigation has found.*

Was it a coincidence that $10 million was exactly how much money Trump had pledged to spend on the campaign from his own fortune?

No charges were brought, according to the *Post*, because during Trump's administration, "prosecutors and FBI agents were blocked by top Justice Department officials from obtaining bank records they believed might hold critical evidence."

There was no evidence that Manafort had anything to do with this alleged, illegal $10 million contribution to Trump's campaign. But it sure looked like a case of history repeating.

Back in 1984, another authoritarian ruler, Ferdinand Marcos of the Philippines, had tried, unsuccessfully, to cling to power by befriending U.S. president Ronald Reagan. Driven into exile by Corazon Aquino's "people power revolution," Marcos and his flamboyant wife, Imelda, fled to Honolulu, Hawaii. (Mrs. Marcos left behind more than three thousand pairs of shoes in her closets.) After a long struggle with kidney disease, Marcos died in exile of cardiac arrest a few years later.

But there was a compelling postscript. In 1991, on a trip to Manila, Edward Rollins, who ran Reagan's 1984 presidential re-election campaign, paid a visit to one of Marcos's cronies. Over lunch at the home of his mistress, the crony said to Rollins: "You ran Reagan's campaign, didn't you?" Rollins nodded. The man continued: "I was the guy who gave the ten million dollars from Marcos to your campaign."

Rollins nearly spit out his host's expensive scotch. He knew nothing about a $10 million campaign contribution and would certainly have remembered receiving that amount. But Rollins played along. He recounted the rest of the conversation in his memoir:

> "*You were the one who gave us that money?*"
> "*Oh, yes,*" *he beamed.* "*I was the guy who made the arrangements and delivered the cash personally . . .*"

"Who did you give the cash to?"

Without batting an eyelash, he gave me the name of a very well-known Washington power lobbyist who was involved in the campaign.

Rollins was stunned. That money, had it ended up in Reagan's reelection coffers, would have constituted an illegal campaign contribution.

Upon his return to the U.S., Rollins went to see Bay Buchanan, who'd been treasurer of Reagan's 1984 reelection race. She assured him that no $10 million contribution had made its way into the campaign's accounts.

In September of 2023, I had lunch with Rollins at an Italian restaurant on New York City's Upper East Side. The veteran GOP campaign manager, 81, a former amateur boxer, was hobbled by Parkinson's disease and physically frail. But he was still mentally acute and eager to talk about past and present political campaigns. When his memoir came out in 1996, Rollins hadn't named the GOP operative who, according to the Marcos crony, had made off with that suitcase full of cash. The operative was then a senior adviser to Bob Dole's presidential bid and Rollins didn't want to torpedo his campaign. But now, over a plate of calamari, Rollins told me who it was: Paul Manafort.

ON A SUNNY MORNING IN AUGUST 2015, JOE BIDEN SUMMONED his inner circle to his home at the Naval Observatory in Northwest Washington, D.C. The question on the table was: Should Biden run against Donald Trump in 2016?

The vice president was reeling from the death just after Memorial Day weekend of his son Beau from brain cancer. It would be a challenge to run a presidential race while shouldering such deep personal grief. Gathered around the pool were Biden's top advisers: his sister, Valerie Biden Owens; longtime confidants Mike Donilon and Steve Ricchetti; political aide Michael Shrum; political director Greg Schultz; and communications aide Kate Bedingfield. Dr. Jill Biden joined them.

The vice president's wound was still raw. "He worried that he'd be on the debate stage and someone would bring up Beau in a way that they shouldn't have," said Schultz. "And he would have walked across the stage and hit somebody."

On the other hand, running for president might be the only way to impart meaning to Beau's death. "Promise me, Dad" was what his son had said to Biden when he was dying—exhorting his father to stay engaged in public life. So Biden kept calling these meetings about running even though his heart wasn't in it. "We just kept running, jumping through hoops," said Schultz. "He wanted someone to talk him out of it. He wanted someone to say, 'You know what? You'd be awesome. It just can't happen anymore.'"

But none of Biden's aides would close that door—so he kept returning to the subject of the 2016 race. A few weeks later, Biden and his brain trust met again. "He kind of went around the table," said an adviser. "There were like seven or eight of us once again. And he was saying he wanted updates on all of these things. 'Where are possible money people? Where are possible allies? Do reporters think there's still a chance?'"

Biden's flirtation with running ended the next day. On October 21, 2015, the vice president joined Barack Obama at a podium in the White House Rose Garden. Flanked by the president and Jill, Biden announced that he would not be a candidate in 2016. He cited the toll Beau's death had taken and said he'd concluded that he was "out of time" to mount a credible campaign.

Yet Biden left little doubt that it pained him to step away. And he took a veiled shot at his rival Hillary Clinton, then running against Vermont senator Bernie Sanders for the nomination; she'd recently called Republicans "enemies." Biden called her out. "I believe we have to end the divisive partisan politics that is ripping this country apart," he said. "I don't think we should look at Republicans as . . . our enemies."

Obama, who'd quietly worked to deliver the nomination to Clinton over his friend and running mate, looked on.

Biden and Obama had a genuine personal bond, forged during Beau's illness. The president had taken Joe under his wing and comforted him; after Beau died and Joe remortgaged his house to pay for some medical bills, Obama offered to write him a check for whatever he needed: "I'll give you the money," the president said. Biden ended up not needing his help.

And yet their relationship had many layers. "I believe that when they say there's a brotherly love, there's also a brotherly competition," said a friend of Biden. A friendship was one thing; a presidential race was another. In assessing his possible successor, Obama was cold-blooded. "We all knew that Biden was much more loyal to Obama than Obama ever was to him," said the friend. This would become painfully apparent to Biden when he ran for reelection in 2024.

In public, Obama promised to give his VP time and space to make his own decision about running in 2016. In private, with the vice president, he was less patient. In his 2017 memoir *Promise Me, Dad,* Biden wrote that when he told Obama he wasn't ready to make up his mind, "the president was not encouraging."

Obama's political advisers were less coy; they didn't think Biden was presidential timber. As one of the vice president's loyalists observed, "the people around Obama never fully understood Biden's appeal to the rest of America. They didn't think he was sophisticated enough. And it's clear that when he ran, a bunch of them were with [Massachusetts Senator] Elizabeth Warren or [South Bend, Indiana] Mayor Pete Buttigieg. They just were dismissive. And they still are. They're just dismissive of Biden's appeal to Middle America."

Obama rubbed salt in Biden's wound when he dispatched his senior adviser David Plouffe to give him advice. Plouffe showed Biden data that forecast an uphill slog to the nomination. Then he said, "Mr. Vice President, you've had a great career, you've been such an asset to this administration—and we love you. Do you really want it to end in a hotel room in Des Moines, coming in third to Bernie Sanders?"

Nothing could have angered Biden more—or made him more determined to show Obama and his condescending advisers just how much they underestimated him.

What particularly rankled Biden and his team was that Obama had been orchestrating Hillary's nomination well before Beau's death. "It was very clear that the machinery inside the party was blessed over to Hillary," said one of Biden's advisers. "They knew what was going on. And they weren't happy about it. That campaign was gearing up in 2014. That was all done before Beau died and with the blessing of Obama."

ON ELECTION NIGHT OF 2016, JOE BIDEN AND HIS WIFE JILL watched Trump's stunning upset over Hillary Clinton. As the "blue wall" of midwestern states flipped to Trump, Biden was sure he would have carried them; they were home to the white working-class voters who'd carried him to victory for years. Biden was certain he would have beaten Trump. Asked later about his decision not to run in 2016, he said, "I regret it every day."

He was already thinking ahead to 2020.

No one seemed more shocked by the 2016 election result than the GOP nominee, who'd watched the returns from Trump Tower in New York City. Earlier that evening, a network producer had called to report that Trump was five points behind in Florida, a critical state. All eyes turned to Susie Wiles, Trump's campaign manager in Florida. She assured them that the sunshine state would go his way. And it did.

Wiles, 59, a veteran GOP operative, knew how to deal with difficult men. Her father, the network sportscaster Pat Summerall, had been an alcoholic, and Wiles had staged family interventions to get him into treatment. She knew something about anger management.

One night in the fall of 2016, enraged by a poll that showed him losing to Hillary Clinton in Florida, Trump had summoned Wiles to his table at his Miami golf resort. How could he be down by so many points, he demanded to know. Trump turned to others at the table. "Do you think she's doing a good job?" he asked them. He turned to Wiles and said, "I don't think you can do this job." To the group Trump said, "Find me someone else." Wiles told him that if he wanted someone to set her "hair on fire," she was not the right person. But "if you want someone to win the state, I can do it."

Wiles got up from the table and returned to her room. But she remained with the campaign. The next time she saw Trump, she told him, "That was nothing short of abuse, and we can't do that again." Trump replied, "We won't have to."

Her ability to withstand abuse would serve Wiles well in 2024—when she'd be tapped to run Trump's presidential campaign.

2

"WHY IS HE RUNNING?"

B y early January of 2019, Joe Biden couldn't wait to run for president of the United States. He'd made no formal decision yet, but at meetings with his aides in the basement of his house in Wilmington, Delaware, the language had morphed from theoretical to real. "All of a sudden," recalled Greg Schultz, his political adviser, "the verb tenses changed. It went from, 'Do we announce our running mate out of the gate?' to 'OK, where will we?' I walked out of one meeting and thought, 'I guess we're doing this!'"

Biden's brain trust consisted of two groups: people who'd been with him for decades, known as the pooh-bahs, and a small band of younger aides. The pooh-bahs included Mike Donilon, 60, Biden's wordsmith and alter ego; Steve Ricchetti, 62, Ron Klain, 58, and Bruce Reed, 59, his former vice-presidential chiefs of staff; Antony Blinken, 57, his ex–national security adviser; and Ted Kaufman, 80, the former senator who was Biden's closest friend. Also in this group were his sister, Valerie Biden Owens, 73, who'd managed Joe's campaigns since he'd run for City Council in 1970, and his wife Jill, 69. Biden's young aides included Schultz and Kate Bedingfield, who were both 38.

And there was one other person who would soon become a powerful member of Biden World. Anita Dunn, 61, a public relations executive, had worked in Barack Obama's White House, specializing in messaging. A newcomer to Biden's inner sanctum, with a cool demeanor and a bob of silver hair, Dunn would become his trusted *consigliere*. She liked to tell people that Biden was the only Irishman who didn't carry a grudge—because she carried them for him. In fact, Biden was a world-class holder of grudges. But Dunn acted on them—clearing obstacles, and people, from his path.

Biden distrusted most of Obama's advisers. Dunn was a rare exception. That was because, for all his resentment of Obama's team, Biden envied their success. "Biden always thinks that smarter people are working for someone else," said a former White House official. "So when Obama's smarter people want to work with him, he thinks, 'Okay, wow, they all like me now.'" To her partnership with Biden, Dunn brought smarts, flattery—and ruthlessness; she was willing to crack heads.

If running for president was too onerous for Joe Biden in 2016, launching a campaign in 2020 arguably made even less sense. After a lifetime of pursuing the brass ring, he'd never come close to grasping it. At 77, he was four years older than Ronald Reagan had been when he showed signs of cognitive decline during his second term.

Moreover, Biden was in the throes of a crisis brought on by his son Hunter's mental illness. Beau's death had pushed Hunter, 49, off the deep end, triggering a steep downward spiral into addiction. In early 2019, as Hunter wrote in his memoir *Beautiful Things*, he was "figuring out how to live when your soul has been ripped from you—when it has been so thoroughly extinguished that you find yourself buying crack in the middle of the night behind a gas station in Nashville, Tennessee . . ."

The last thing a father needed, with his son in the midst of a life-and-death struggle, was a presidential campaign. Even for Biden, who'd been around this track twice before, it would require a single-minded focus at the expense of everything else. And a presidential race would bring otherworldly levels of stress and scrutiny. And yet Joe Biden wanted to run. Why?

Part of it was Biden's genuine outrage at Trump's reaction to the white supremacist rally at Charlottesville, Virginia, on August 11, 2017; he'd remarked that there were "very fine people on both sides." And yet it didn't fully explain why Biden was running.

In his book on the 1988 campaign, *What It Takes,* Richard Ben Cramer posed the essential question for would-be presidents: "Who are these guys? . . . What in their backgrounds could give them that huge ambition, that kind of motor, that will and discipline, that faith in themselves? What kind of faith would cause . . . [them] to bend their lives and the lives of those dear to them to one hugely public roll of the dice in which all but one would fail?"

The answer was that Joe Biden had something to prove. He would show everyone who doubted him, including Obama and his advisers, just how wrong they were. Biden was convinced that he had a unique bond with the working American middle class. Those corny stories about Scranton Joe and his dad's sayings at the kitchen table weren't just bromides; he really believed them. And as the 2020 campaign would prove, Biden did have a special connection with blue-collar voters in battleground states. "People would talk about FDR Democrats, Kennedy Democrats," said Schultz, "but we should be talking about Biden Democrats." Biden believed he was uniquely qualified to run against Trump in 2020. He wasn't sure anyone else could beat him.

MEANWHILE, DONALD TRUMP WAS PREPARING TO RUN FOR RE-election against Joe Biden. And so were his closest advisers.

By the spring of 2018, two people were first among equals in Trump's White House: Jared and Ivanka Kushner. The president's son-in-law and daughter, who'd left New York City to become senior advisers in her father's West Wing, were involved in almost everything—from trade deals to economic entrepreneurship to criminal justice reform to Middle East diplomacy. And they would be key figures in his 2020 reelection campaign.

I got my first glimpse into the world of "Javanka" in the summer of 2018, when I paid a visit to their home in Washington, D.C.

On May 21, I'd received an unexpected email from Ivanka's assistant at the White House: She said that Ivanka had read my book *The Gatekeepers*, a history of the White House chiefs of staff, published the previous year, and had found it "incredibly relevant." Would I meet with her so that she could learn more?

Since my book's release in March 2017, I was often asked to speak to groups interested in White House governance. But this invitation threw me. *The Gatekeepers* was scrupulously nonpartisan in its treatment of White House chiefs on both sides of the aisle. But as a frequent guest on cable news programs, I'd been blunt about my view of Donald Trump's White House: It was a disaster, the most dysfunctional in modern history. So I viewed this invitation with a mixture of curiosity and trepidation.

Early on a Friday evening, I went to the Kushners' home in the affluent Kalorama section of Northwest Washington, D.C.

My wife and I took an Uber and, at Jared's suggestion, got out at a spot behind the house—to avoid the *Daily Mail* photographer staked out across from their front door. The three-level home was surrounded by cypress trees. A Secret Service agent led us to a ground-floor garage, where we climbed the steps to the first landing. We were greeted in the kitchen by Ivanka's personal assistant, who was playing with the couple's toddler, Joseph.

From the next landing, Ivanka called out warmly, "Thanks so much for coming." She wore a white dress embroidered with black flowers and a black choker. A butler asked for our drink order and we took a seat across from her on the couch.

Ivanka was gracious and charming but got right to the point. "It's so interesting to learn that other White Houses had the same kind of chaos we had during our first year," she said. (Well, not *that* much chaos, I was tempted to reply.) Ivanka wanted to know more. After a few minutes, she looked up and over my shoulder. Jared had arrived from the White House. Wearing a blue shirt with a monogram *JCK* and gold cuff links, he shook our hands and then slipped onto the love seat beside Ivanka. They held hands.

The Kushners peppered me with questions about presidents, their chiefs of staff, and the way a White House should be run. Ivanka enjoyed hearing stories of backstabbing and infighting in previous administrations. When it came to turmoil and dysfunction in the White House, she seemed relieved to know they were not alone.

That evening was the first of many visits I paid to the Kushners over the next three years. Our conversations, in person and over the phone, were conducted, at Jared's insistence, mostly off the record. What was *his* agenda? I concluded that Jared was looking for advice on how to navigate a White House riven by internecine strife.

From the day he set foot in the West Wing, Kushner had been battling with rivals for Trump's ear. Steve Bannon, Trump's chief political strategist, and Reince Priebus, his White House chief of staff, had joined forces and tried to force Jared out. Bannon blamed him for almost every Trump blunder, including the firing of FBI Director James Comey on May 9, 2017. That move, supported by Jared, had led to the appointment of Special Counsel Robert Mueller and his probe of the Trump campaign's alleged collusion with Russia. For his part, Priebus resented Jared and Ivanka's unfettered access to the president.

But neither Priebus nor Bannon was family and Trump had grown weary of both men. On July 28, 2017, as his chief of staff stood on the tarmac next to Air Force One, Trump tweeted the news of Priebus's departure. Bannon's sacking came less than a month later; he'd angered Trump with his constant leaking and self-promotion, including an appearance on the cover of *TIME*.

Now, in July of 2018, Jared and Ivanka had taken aim at another antagonist: John Kelly. He was the ramrod-straight, no-nonsense, four-star Marine Corps general who'd replaced Priebus as White House chief of staff. The Kushners despised Kelly; not only had he tried to impose discipline on the West Wing, thereby restricting their Oval Office access, but he'd yanked Jared's top-secret security clearance. (Kushner's background check had evidently been flagged because of his foreign business entanglements.) Jared and Ivanka were determined to get rid of Kelly; indeed, they asked me for advice on his replacement. The retired general would last seventeen months; on January 2, 2019, Trump fired Kelly and replaced him with "acting chief" Mick Mulvaney, a former South Carolina congressman and OMB director. But Kelly would return to become a thorn in Trump's side during the 2024 election.

In the meantime, there was a reelection campaign to run.

FOR THE JOB OF MANAGING TRUMP'S 2020 REELECTION CAM-paign, it would be hard to imagine a more outlandish character than Brad Parscale. Six feet eight inches tall, tattooed and bearded, Parscale was a character out of a Carl Hiaasen novel. As the digital director of Trump's 2016 campaign, he was credited with discovering hard-to-reach MAGA supporters and driving them to the polls. But Parscale answered to the beat of his own drum. Instead of working out of campaign headquarters in Washington, D.C., he set up shop by the pool at his waterfront home in Fort Lauderdale, Florida, where he could soak up the sun with his two Australian Labradoodles.

In February 2018, with Jared's encouragement, Trump put Parscale in charge of his reelection campaign. It was partly because the architects of the 2016 race were unavailable. Bannon had been sent into exile. Kushner had soured on Kellyanne Conway, who was then serving as a White House adviser.

And Paul Manafort was on his way to prison.

On July 31, 2018, Manafort went to trial in the first of two prosecutions brought by Robert Mueller's team. The first trial, in Virginia, was for tax and bank fraud charges. The second, in Washington, D.C., was for violations of the Foreign Agents Registration Act (FARA), money laundering, tax conspiracy, lying, and witness tampering. Manafort was convicted on eight counts in the first trial. Just before the second got underway, he agreed to cooperate with the prosecution.

But Manafort had not "flipped" on Trump. Instead of telling

prosecutors everything he knew, he breached his agreement by repeatedly lying to them before a federal grand jury. Trump's former campaign chairman would end up being sentenced to 7½ years in prison. But Manafort had an ace up his sleeve: a presidential pardon.

ALTHOUGH PARSCALE WAS THE NOMINAL 2020 CAMPAIGN MANager, he reported to Jared. Parscale was a wizard at digital data and technology, but few regarded him as a campaign strategist. "Height is not depth," quipped Kellyanne Conway.

And sure enough, Parscale would soon be in trouble. A lavish shopping spree would give Trump and Kushner an excuse to fire him.

THE AMOUNT OF MONEY SPENT ON U.S. PRESIDENTIAL RACES IS mind-bending. In 2020, the Trump and Biden campaigns would end up spending nearly $3 billion. And that was just *their* money; when you included so-called independent expenditures (i.e.s) by super PACs and other parties, the total spending on the 2020 race came to an estimated $14 billion. Given the vast sums involved, campaign strategists and digital directors can make a killing. They do it by pocketing a fee—often between 8 and 10 percent of television ad buys that can run as high as eight figures.

Exactly how much Parscale was earning as Trump's 2020 campaign manager isn't clear; he insisted that he drew a flat salary of $360,000. But Parscale was living so high off the hog that he made Manafort look frugal.

In 2019, a news story reported that Parscale had been buying up Florida waterfront condos and luxury cars. Trump called Parscale into his office. "What the fuck?" he yelled at his campaign manager. "I just hate these fucking stories."

Jared came to Parscale's defense, calling him a good investment. "Brad can make a million fucking dollars a month with his marketing skills," he told Trump. "And, by the way, I'd be the first person to hire him. You're getting him for $30,000 a month. So you need to just calm down."

But it was the calm before another storm of bad publicity. The *Daily Mail* reported that Parscale had scarfed up vacation houses, boats, and a bright red Ferrari. His profligate ways caught the attention of the Lincoln Project, an organization run by Republicans-turned–Never Trumpers. Before you could say "Lamborghini," the Lincoln Project had created a television spot about Parscale. Released on May 20, 2019, it was aimed at triggering Trump: "Meet Brad Parscale," announced the narrator, "from dead broke to the man Trump can't win without. Brad is getting rich. How rich? Really rich!"

The ad cut to a beautiful model putting her finger up to her lips. The narrator continued: "But don't tell Donald. He'd wonder how Brad can afford so much: a $2.4 million waterfront house in Fort Lauderdale. Two Florida condos worth almost a million each. He even has his very own yacht, a gorgeous Ferrari, a sleek Range Rover. Brad brags about using private jets. Oh, my! Brad's a star! And why not? Brad's worth every dollar. Just ask him!"

One can only imagine the slow burn Trump experienced as he watched that ad. Parscale insisted he was misunderstood; all that Florida booty was paid for with millions he'd earned from selling his businesses in San Antonio. The spending spree, Parscale said, was his way of coping with a family tragedy; he and his wife had suffered the sudden death of newborn twins. Still, by the spring of 2019, Parscale's head was on Trump's chopping block.

On April 25, 2019, Joe Biden released a video announcing his candidacy for president of the United States. He joined a scrum of twenty-six other candidates vying for the nomination, including senators Kamala Harris, Cory Booker, Elizabeth Warren, Amy Klobuchar, and Bernie Sanders (from California, New Jersey, Massachusetts, Minnesota, and Vermont, respectively). Pete Buttigieg, mayor of South Bend, Indiana, and Beto O'Rourke, a charismatic young congressman from Texas, rounded out the field.

O'Rourke's campaign manager was a young woman named Jennifer O'Malley Dillon, universally known as JOD. She reportedly greeted the news of Biden's candidacy with the crack: "Why is he running?" It was a slight heard around the campaign world.

But over the next few months, Biden held his own in eleven debates with his rivals. It was a bumpy road to the nomination—and the first big hurdle was the Iowa Caucus. A burial ground for many presidential candidates, the caucus, scheduled for February 3, 2020, tended to reward liberal activists, not centrists like Biden. It required enormous effort, organization, and money. The New Hampshire primary, which came just eight days later, on February 11, was also unfriendly terrain for Biden. Sanders and Warren, from neighboring Vermont and Massachusetts, were favored there over the former vice president.

If Biden could endure losses in Iowa and New Hampshire, he'd live to fight another day—on the much friendlier turf of South Carolina, with its heavy concentration of African-American voters. If he could win the primary there, on February 29, the campaign would become a two-person race between Biden and Sanders, leader of the party's progressives. In the Super Tuesday primaries that followed, on March 3, the moderate wing of the Democratic Party would unite behind Biden as the nominee.

That was the plan, but Biden evidently never got the memo. His longtime political adviser, Greg Schultz, who was managing his nascent 2020 presidential campaign, tried to warn the boss that he was headed for a drubbing in Iowa and New Hampshire. But the pooh-bahs—along with Biden's old Senate pal John Kerry and former Ohio governor Tom Vilsack—kept assuring the candidate, without evidence, that things were looking good: Why, he might even finish first in Iowa!

So Biden was dismayed when he was trounced in Iowa, finishing a distant fourth. Enter Anita Dunn. "He was floundering," said a campaign staffer. "And she just stepped in and started managing. She proved herself to him because she just took over. She just stepped up and made decisions."

One of Dunn's decisions was to order everyone to depart for South Carolina even before the New Hampshire returns came in. (That proved wise—because Biden finished a dismal fifth there and didn't have to answer questions.) Another Dunn decision was to sack Schultz as campaign manager.

She replaced him with Jen O'Malley Dillon, Beto O'Rourke's ambitious and sometimes abrasive campaign manager. (O'Rourke had dropped out of the race on November 1.) Dunn was willing to overlook O'Malley Dillon's earlier wisecrack about Biden—because she was just what he needed. Whip-smart and tenacious, she was an organizational genius.

She was also a suffer-no-fools badass. As one campaign veteran put it: "Some people wake up every day and say, 'Oh, I've got to get these things done today.' Jen wakes up and says 'Someone fucked up. I'm going to find out who it was and make him pay for it.'" It paid to tread carefully around O'Malley Dillon. "I know a staff member who she scared out of a gym once," said a campaign operative. "She didn't want somebody to be on the treadmill next to her, so she just glowered at them until they left." Her brutal verbal takedowns of staffers were legendary; one subordinate burst into tears after being chewed out by her. And she was one of O'Malley Dillon's best friends.

Biden and his team couldn't wait for South Carolina at the end of February—where the candidate could tap into his core constituency: Black voters. The campaign had done a focus group in the state with Black women, aged 50 to 70; it was eye-opening. A major takeaway was that Biden got enormous credit for having been Obama's loyal VP. A typical comment was "I've never seen a white man stand behind a Black man for eight years and never once undercut him."

On February 29, 2020, buoyed by the endorsement of Congressman James Clyburn, Biden won the South Carolina primary in a rout, with 48.6 percent of the vote. Sanders was a distant second with 19.8 percent. Declared politically dead by nearly every pundit just a month earlier, Biden had risen from the grave.

In South Carolina's aftermath, O'Malley Dillon and Dunn were touted as geniuses. And Dunn was now shaping Biden's engagement with the world. "Anita controlled everything," said an aide, "everything related to press, to community, to strategic communications, to branding, to messaging, to who the president sat down with, to town halls, to when to deny *Meet the Press* and *Face the Nation* an interview. This was all Anita."

Dunn's posture toward the media was almost Nixonian in its insularity and hostility. There was no "enemies list" because almost everyone in the press would have been on it—starting with

The New York Times. On Dunn's watch, few interviews would be granted to mainstream media. Her attitude, said a colleague, was "We've got a guy who's prone to mistakes so we're just not going to do that shit." Lack of transparency would become a hallmark of Biden's White House. And it would ultimately hurt the president when his party turned against him in 2024.

IN EARLY 2020, DONALD TRUMP COULDN'T BELIEVE HIS TERRI-ble luck. From the moment the alarm was sounded in January about a dangerous new virus called COVID-19, he'd tried to deny its existence. In Trump's mind, he'd been cruising comfortably toward reelection. And now he was being sabotaged by some kind of Democrat or Chinese hoax.

The outbreak of the COVID-19 pandemic instantly upended Trump's campaign. In early February 2020, Parscale had been telling the boss that he was headed for a Ronald Reagan–style landslide. (In 1984, Reagan carried forty-nine states to win a second term against Democrat Walter F. Mondale.) "I mean, we were within the margin of error in Oregon, New Mexico, and New Hampshire," Parscale recalled, citing three solidly Democratic-leaning states. "I had never seen polling that good. We were up six, seven, eight points on a Biden ticket. I remember we were looking at 340-plus electoral votes before COVID."

By the spring of 2020, Parscale was singing a different tune. Battered by his fumbling of the pandemic, Trump was headed for defeat. This was not what the president wanted to hear.

AS THE SUMMER OF 2020 NEARED, BIDEN FACED A CRITICAL question: Who would be his running mate? On a cross-country flight, he'd once remarked to an aide: "There are some really good women who would be good vice presidents." One of Biden's early favorites was Michigan governor Gretchen Whitmer. "When she endorsed him for president, he fell in love with her instantly," said the aide. But Biden's infatuation faded before practical political considerations. On August 11, 2020, he chose Kamala Harris.

At first glance Harris was a surprising pick. Memorably, in their primary debate on June 27, 2019, Harris had knocked Biden on his heels with a roundhouse punch: a pointed, personal attack on his opposition to school busing to achieve integration back in the 1970s. But Biden got over it. He believed he needed a person of color on his ticket. And Harris was a silver-tongued prosecutor who could be counted on to dominate Trump's vice president Mike Pence in a debate. There was one other thing, intangible but invaluable in Biden World. Harris had been close to Beau when they served as attorneys general in California and Delaware, respectively.

AS TRUMP'S REELECTION TEAM ENTERED THE FINAL LAP, suddenly the wheels came off.

On Sunday, July 12, 2020, *The Washington Post* ran a front-page story: "Trump Frustrated with Campaign Manager Parscale Amid Falling Polls." The article reported that Parscale had cast himself as the star of a campaign television ad. It also noted that during the critical final days of the primary, Parscale was working poolside in Florida.

Just a month earlier, Trump had been embarrassed when Parscale boasted that almost a million MAGA supporters had applied for tickets to a campaign rally in Tulsa, Oklahoma. It turned out that thousands of anti-MAGA pranksters on Tik-Tok had reserved tickets—and almost no one showed up. But Trump's problem with Parscale was more fundamental. "My message to him during COVID was: You're losing and we must change course," Parscale told me. "And he didn't like hearing that. He couldn't believe he was losing to Biden."

On Wednesday, July 15, Jared called Parscale into his office. "Brad, you're being demoted," he told him. Parscale was being reassigned to his old job as digital director.

Parscale flew straight home to Fort Lauderdale. Thirty-six days before the election, the police received a 911 call from his house. Parscale and his wife had been drinking and fighting. When the cops pulled into the driveway, she was outside, with visible bruises on her arms and legs. She said that Parscale had been threatening to harm himself. And there were guns in the house.

What happened next was captured on video and spread quickly on social media. Standing with his wife in his driveway, shirtless and shoeless and clutching a beer, Parscale was tackled and thrown to the ground by a cop. Trump's ex–campaign manager was taken to a psychiatric facility for evaluation.

Trump called Kellyanne Conway. "Can you believe this guy?" he said. "He is so weak. I had to get rid of him. A dumbass. Did you see him in that video with the police? With the beer shirt on the lawn? And the whole wife thing? That was horrible!"

Kellyanne replied: "Well, actually, Mr. President, he had a beer can in his hand and no shirt."

With just a month to go before the election, Bill Stepien, a Kushner protégé who'd served as Trump's White House political director, was now the campaign manager, reporting to Jared. There was no time to waste.

Trump had bungled the pandemic. He'd mismanaged the crisis—undermining scientists, refusing to wear a mask, and baldly asserting, without evidence, that bleach injections might be a cure. (Trump had at least managed to put the country on a fast track to developing a vaccine.) By contrast, Biden preached respect for facts, science, and expertise. But the pandemic offered Biden a tactical campaign advantage as well.

To avoid getting COVID, Biden drastically curtailed his public appearances. Trump accused him of "hiding in his basement." And indeed, as Biden's aides would later confess, when interviewing a candidate to run the 2024 race, campaigning from home gave Biden a twofold advantage: He could hide the fact that he was a lackluster campaigner—and that his events didn't draw big crowds. Campaigning from his basement, Biden could phone it in. And there was a third advantage to campaigning from the basement. Biden was aging dramatically. He wasn't up to the rigors of a traditional campaign.

COVID was one factor that doomed Trump's reelection. Another was the candidate himself. No matter how much Kushner and Stepien tried to keep him focused on the issues, Trump did his own thing. He talked about how the election would be rigged and staged divisive stunts like his tone-deaf, strongman march to Lafayette Square in June 2020 (where he preened with an upside-down Bible). "Welcome to every campaign manager that he's ever had," Parscale told me. "That's just what he is—his own campaign manager."

In late September, I visited Jared at the White House. By this time the West Wing had become a COVID incubator, a hothouse of potential contagion. But few people wore masks in the cramped confines of the West Wing. Meeting with Jared in his small, windowless cubicle just off the Oval Office, I asked him what he thought of the president's prospects. Kushner had reportedly told Trump that despite dismal polling, internal campaign data showed that he could win. Jared told me he was confident in Trump's ground game. But he didn't sound convinced.

On November 3, 2020, election night, Kushner, Stepien, Ivanka, and the rest of the campaign staff gathered in the White House's Map Room to monitor the returns. At 11:04 p.m., Fox News declared that Trump would carry Florida—another win by Susie Wiles that the president would not forget. The trends looked good in Ohio, another must-win state. But soon everything changed.

At 11:21 p.m., Fox News interrupted its pundits with an urgent update: With 73 percent of the votes counted, the network projected that Biden would win Arizona. If true, this was a disaster for Trump. It would dramatically narrow his path to victory.

As the evening wore on, it was clear to almost everyone except Trump that he was headed to defeat. At 2:20 a.m., the president strode defiantly to the podium in the White House's East Room: "This is a fraud on the American public," he said. "This is an embarrassment to our country. We were getting ready to win this election. Frankly, we did win this election."

Biden had won the popular vote by seven million, but the all-important electoral college was razor-close. The election was decided by just 44,000 votes in Georgia, Arizona, and Wisconsin.

With his attorneys Rudy Giuliani and Sidney Powell, Trump would soon embark on his campaign to stop what he called "the Big Steal." But Trump would have to fight that battle without Kushner. His son-in-law was not only the de facto campaign manager but a virtual secretary of state without portfolio; he was headed to the Middle East to work on a deal to resolve a blockade of Qatar by Saudi Arabia, Bahrain, Egypt, and the United Arab Emirates.

On January 6, 2021, returning from Saudi Arabia, Kushner landed at Joint Base Andrews at 3 p.m. The violent assault by a MAGA mob on the U.S. Capitol was underway.

The Secret Service took Jared to his home in Kalorama.

By the time Kushner arrived at the White House, just after 4 p.m., the president had finally released a video telling the MAGA crowd to go home.

Two weeks later, on the morning of January 20, 2021, with American flags flapping behind him, Donald Trump addressed a small band of supporters at Joint Base Andrews, on his way to Air Force One. He made his intentions clear. "Goodbye, we love you," he said. "We will be back in some form."

"EVERY FREAKING ONE OF THEM HAD NO BALLS."

On a balmy evening in February 2021, Donald Trump invited Susie Wiles to join him for dinner on his Mar-a-Lago patio. Mild-mannered and soft-spoken, Wiles, 64, a grandmother, brought along a detailed after-action report on Florida, the state she'd helped him win in 2016 and 2020. But Wiles hadn't come just to talk about Florida. There was a reason Trump had lost the presidential election in 2020, she told him. It was because his campaign had been flying blind. States had been organized by people who didn't know the terrain. If Trump wanted to win in 2024, he would need to replicate nationwide what she had done in Florida.

Wiles was a creature of the GOP. She'd had her start in 1979, when, just out of the University of Maryland, she landed a job in the Capitol Hill office of Jack Kemp, the pro quarterback–turned–conservative Republican congressman from New York. The job had been arranged by her father, the ex–New York Giants football player and legendary television sportscaster Pat Summerall. Later, Wiles worked as a scheduler in Ronald Reagan's White House. She married a Reagan advance man, Lanny Wiles, and moved to Florida's Ponte Vedra Beach.

It was in Florida that Wiles mastered her craft as a campaign operative. In the 1990s and 2000s, working for two centrist Republican mayors of Jacksonville, she earned a reputation as a savvy organizer with extensive connections to players throughout the state. Wiles signed on to John McCain's presidential campaign and then managed Rick Scott's winning race for Florida governor. But it was in 2018 that her career took a fateful turn, when she connected with an ambitious Florida politician named Ron DeSantis. Wiles managed his winning 2018 campaign for governor. "The governor would not be the governor if not for Susie Wiles," said a DeSantis staffer to *Politico Magazine*. But Wiles soon discovered that no good deed goes unpunished.

DeSantis and his wife, Casey, turned against Wiles. Their reasons were opaque; they were reported to have suspected her of claiming credit for the governor's victory or leaking a damaging story about him. In any event, in the summer of 2019, at DeSantis's behest, Trump told Parscale to fire Wiles. "He said, 'Brad, let her go nicely' and I did," recalled Parscale. "I called her on the phone, which I tried to avoid doing for months, and let her go. I tried to soften the news by saying, 'Someday I'll probably work for you. That's how Trump World works.'" But a year later, sinking in the Florida polls, Trump decided to bring Wiles back. He called DeSantis to tell him. "She won Florida for me," Trump said. "Well," replied DeSantis, "that's like saying the bat boy won the World Series for you."

Trump brushed off DeSantis. And he rehired Wiles.

According to Conway, Wiles was a combination of Zen tactician and NFL running back: "She's calm. She doesn't swear. She doesn't raise her voice. I think she looked at her job as moving mud. To use a Pat Summerall football analogy, she was happy to get three yards and a cloud of dust in between a couple of successful Hail Marys for every single week and month."

Wiles and Trump were an odd couple. She was an old-school, establishment Republican with impeccable manners. He was a political wrecking ball who played by his own rules. Her mentors had been Ronald Reagan and John McCain. His was the ruthless lawyer Roy Cohn. As Wiles wrote in an email later published in *The New York Times*: "As a card-carrying member of the GOP establishment, many thought my full-throated endorsement of the Trump candidacy was ill-advised—even crazy."

"Crazy" was a polite word for what many of her GOP friends thought; they were appalled by her embrace of an authoritarian election-denier. But in the winter of 2021, as she dined with Trump at Mar-a-Lago and talked about the upcoming race, Wiles had her reasons, both personal and professional, for embracing the former president. She'd recently been divorced. And thanks to DeSantis's vendetta, her job prospects were murky. Finally, whether it was delusional thinking or genuine conviction or both, Wiles told people that she knew the real Trump. A Trump who, she insisted, would always do the right thing.

Wiles and Trump had something in common. Both had been raised by difficult fathers. Fred Trump, the real estate developer from Queens, was a cold-hearted man who denied his children emotional support. Pat Summerall, who became the mellifluous voice of the NFL, was an absent father, a philanderer, and an alcoholic. In his 2008 memoir, *On and Off the Air*, Summerall credited his daughter with leading family interventions that got him to seek treatment.

Although Trump didn't drink, he had his own addictions—to money, power, and fame. "She is an expert in unstable, dysfunctional, famous men," said Mac Stipanovich, a veteran Tallahassee GOP operative. "She knows when she can help, and she knows when not to try to help."

Children of alcoholics develop extraordinary coping mechanisms; they learn how to navigate chaos. There would be plenty of that for Wiles to navigate in the campaign to come.

During that February dinner at Mar-a-Lago, Trump asked Wiles to run his super PAC "Save America." She readily agreed. Two weeks later, he invited her back. Trump wanted Wiles to organize his political life. Word began to spread that there was a chief of staff at Mar-a-Lago.

FROM HIS FIRST DAY IN OFFICE, JOE BIDEN WAS AS TIGHTLY scripted as any president in modern history. Anita Dunn had passed up a West Wing office and returned to her Washington, D.C., public relations firm, SKDK. But even from afar, she remained completely in charge of the president's communications. Her modus operandi was to hide him from the press.

In shielding Biden from the media, Dunn was pushing on an open door. For all his back-slapping bonhomie when he was a senator, Biden was deeply wary of reporters. The derailment of his 1988 presidential campaign, when accusations of plagiarism drove him from the race, had left a lasting wound.

Jill Biden was also particularly scarred by the experience. "What drove her to Joe in the first place," said a friend, "was his integrity and his strength—that he was outwardly principled and a gentleman in the classic sense. It stung her so much to see his integrity questioned. She was devastated. From that point on, she became much more aware and mistrustful of the press."

The isolation of the forty-sixth president had begun.

During his first year in office, only Ronald Reagan gave fewer White House press conferences. Bucking tradition, Biden gave no interviews to *The New York Times* or *The Washington Post*. Dunn and her team routinely turned down invitations from the major network Sunday news programs.

Even Biden's acquaintances were kept at bay. Bill Daley, former White House chief of staff to Barack Obama, paid frequent visits to one of the president's senior advisers in the West Wing. "I went to the White House a dozen times," he told me. "Never once did somebody say, 'Oh, come on in and see the president.' Never. Everything was scripted."

A former high-ranking aide thought that walling Biden off from the world was a grave mistake. "They were afraid he might say the wrong thing or might feed the mental acuity narrative," he told me. "And so he started to see fewer and fewer people. They allowed his faculties to atrophy. But I think, like knives, they have to be sharpened. They get sharpened by rubbing them up against steel. And they don't get sharpened by sitting in the drawer."

By November 2021, nine months into his presidency, Joe Biden had good reason to forego a reelection race. After the bungled evacuation of Afghanistan, his approval rating, once above 50 percent, had plummeted; it had dipped as low as the high 30s—an almost Trumpian level. The country was still battered by COVID variants, supply-chain problems, and the highest inflation in nearly forty years. And then there was Biden's age.

Biden had hinted that he might be a one-term president. Back in December 2019, *Politico* had reported that he and his advisers had discussed making a pledge not to seek a second term. "It is virtually inconceivable," *Politico* reported, "that he will run for reelection in 2024, when he would be the first octogenarian president." Then, in March 2020, sharing a stage with a new generation of Democratic leaders—Michigan governor Gretchen Whitmer, California senator Kamala Harris, and New Jersey senator Cory Booker—Biden proclaimed: "Look, I view myself as a bridge, not as anything else."

Biden would later suggest that his plan to pass the torch had been thwarted by events. "What happened was we were having so much success getting things done," he said on the television program *The View*, in September 2024. "I found myself having used more time . . ." In other words, he was too busy being president to groom a successor.

But the evidence suggests that Biden planned to run for reelection all along. His inner circle dismissed the alternative. "This whole thing about him serving one term, I don't remember any discussions of that," said Ted Kaufman, Biden's close friend. "I mean, committing to only serve one term is a BFD." In Kaufman's view, forsaking a second term was not only a Big Fucking Deal, it made no sense. "I don't think it's ever happened before and he was in great shape. He knew what he was doing and presidents run for two terms."

Another factor spurred Biden to run again: the continuing threat of Trump. According to his White House chief of staff, Ron Klain, what shocked Biden more than anything else during his presidency was Trump's lasting power. Having won the 2020 election by seven million votes, Biden was convinced he had a mandate. Trump and his movement, he thought, would fade in the rearview mirror. And yet even after two failed impeachments, a bloody attempted insurrection, and a criminal conviction, Trump wasn't going anywhere.

Biden doubted anyone else could beat Trump in 2024. And as in 2020, the stakes couldn't be higher; this race would be another battle for the soul of the nation. His vice president, Kamala Harris, had struggled in the job—privately, to a friend, Biden had called her "a work in progress." And her approval rating, 36 percent, was even lower than Biden's.

So the president and his advisers put out the word that he would seek his party's nomination in 2024. The public announcement could wait—but privately Biden wanted Democrats to know that the president would employ all the powers of incumbency to defeat any rivals in 2024. The message was: Don't even think about challenging me.

There was just one problem. Biden was aging rapidly and everyone around him knew it.

On June 24, 2022, the United States Supreme Court overturned *Roe v. Wade* and stripped women of their constitutional right to an abortion. Months before the court handed down its decision in *Dobbs v. Jackson Women's Health Organization*, *Politico* published a leaked draft of Justice Samuel Alito's opinion. That night, Kamala Harris spoke at a gala dinner for EMILYs List. "Those Republican leaders who are trying to weaponize the use of the law against women—well, we say, 'How dare they?'" she thundered. "How dare they tell a woman what she can and cannot do with her own body?"

When the Dobbs decision was announced, Donald Trump was in his office at his golf club in Bedminster, New Jersey. Sitting across from him was Chris LaCivita, a veteran GOP operative from Virginia whom Trump was thinking of hiring for his nascent campaign. A Marine with a shaved head and the build of an offensive tackle, LaCivita was known as a straight shooter. "Mr. President," he said, upon hearing the news, "you just did what a lot of people have never been able to do. You overturned Roe v. Wade."

Indeed, Trump had done just that; the polarizing 6–3 decision had been made possible by his appointment of three conservative Supreme Court justices, Neil Gorsuch, Brett Kavanaugh, and Amy Coney Barrett. In the 2022 midterm elections, the Dobbs ruling would become a lethal political weapon against Republicans, helping Democrats defy expectations.

LaCivita was another larger-than-life character among Trump's campaigners. He drank whiskey, smoked cigars, and had been known to fire a shotgun at birds while talking to reporters on his cell phone. He'd served in the Gulf War, where he was wounded by shrapnel and won a Purple Heart. Afterward, LaCivita had gone to work for George Allen, a congressman, senator, and governor from Virginia.

LaCivita would always go the extra mile for a candidate; in 1992, during Allen's race for governor, he swam a hundred yards across an icy lake to plant a campaign sign on an island. But LaCivita became best known, in 2004, for creating a devastating television ad campaign against John Kerry, the Democratic presidential nominee. LaCivita's "Swift Boat Veterans for Truth"—which featured Vietnam veterans denouncing Kerry's military record—helped to sink his campaign and reelect George W. Bush.

The Swift Boats campaign was widely denounced for the lies it told about Kerry's Vietnam service. But to many Republicans it was considered the touchstone of negative advertising.

LaCivita was introduced to Trump World in 2020, when Karl Rove, George W. Bush's former chief strategist, got a phone call from Sheldon Adelson, the billionaire casino magnate. Adelson wanted to give Trump $100 million—and asked Rove to take charge of spending it. Rove demurred and suggested he put the money in a Trump-affiliated super PAC run by LaCivita. It ended up being called Preserve America.

Trump's pollster Tony Fabrizio suggested to Susie Wiles that she hire LaCivita to help run the 2024 campaign. That led to dinners with Wiles and that visit with Trump at his club in Bedminster. In October 2022, the former president hired LaCivita as a senior adviser, working alongside Wiles. But she would be first among equals.

Trump's hiring of LaCivita caught the GOP establishment off-guard. "I'm surprised because I know what he thinks of Trump," said Rove. "He thinks Trump's an idiot." Privately, to friends, LaCivita had slammed Trump's role in fomenting the January 6 insurrection; on Twitter he'd shared a post by George W. Bush calling the assault "a sickening and heartbreaking sight." But LaCivita eventually succumbed to Wiles's blandishments and the chance to co-manage a presidential campaign. Given his feelings about Trump's recklessness, the question remained: Would LaCivita try to *manage* Trump? Could he tell the candidate what he didn't want to hear?

"I'm very confident," said Rove, "that there probably have been four or five instances when he's told Trump to go f--- himself and walked out of the room. He is a tough guy. He doesn't take shit. And my sense is that Trump on the one hand doesn't like that, and on the other hand admires it." Rove wasn't betting on LaCivita's longevity. "I'm surprised he's lasted as long as he has," he told me in January of 2024. "I think he and Susie have done an incredible job of managing probably the ultimate difficult candidate."

Wiles and LaCivita were touted in the political press as game changers. "Two of America's most feared political operatives," *The Atlantic* called them. They were portrayed as consummate campaign professionals—the antidote to the amateurs who'd run Trump's 2016 and 2020 races. According to this theory, Trump had won in 2016 despite being managed by a clown car of bumblers, and he'd lost in 2020 because no competent person had been in charge. By contrast, Trump's 2024 campaign would be a juggernaut, a Democrat's nightmare. "Inside the Terrifyingly Competent Trump 2024 Campaign" read one headline in April 2024. A subhead in a *Vanity Fair* piece, aimed at Democrats, asked, "How worried should you be? Very."

But not everyone was impressed. Kellyanne Conway argued that the 2016 campaign was the benchmark, a view she said Trump shared. "He looks at the 2016 crew as winners," she said. "And as very bold, having hunger and swagger and being underdogs, underestimated, resolute, impervious to all the criticisms and naysayers and the fiction of un-electability." And if Trump's first presidential campaign team was such a bunch of losers, how come he won?

I was struck by Conway's self-assurance, her certainty that she occupied a special place in Trump's orbit. The day before we spoke, September 17, 2024, in a piece about Corey Lewandowski, *The New York Times* reported, "Mr. Trump is agitated that few members of the 2016 team remain in the campaign's inner circle." So I asked Conway, Did Trump miss her? "He does miss me, but he gets a lot of me and I get a lot of him," she replied, referring to their frequent phone conversations. And she wasn't the only member of the 2016 campaign gang that Trump missed. Before long even the most discredited OGs from 2016— Corey Lewandowski and Paul Manafort, who'd been banished and imprisoned, respectively—would join the 2024 campaign. But since they still despised each other, they could never be in the same room.

Another veteran of Trump's 2016 race, who preferred to be anonymous, questioned the 2024 campaign managers' allegiance. Of LaCivita, she said, "Anybody that hated Trump should not be at the top of his campaign. Period. That's just a no-brainer. Even Susie didn't support Trump in the beginning. So if the team making the decisions are not invested in you, how do you win? You're probably not going to win."

Some people believed LaCivita was behind stories trashing Trump and praising his handlers. "Chris talks to the Washington–New York media all day," said a 2016 campaign veteran. "And Trump is like, 'Oh, he leaks the good stuff.' We're like, 'No. Here are all the stories that say the campaign is disciplined and poised to win, but the candidate's not.' That, to me, is like a fireable offense."

In November of 2022, Joe Biden appeared to be on the ropes.

As the midterm elections approached, the conventional wisdom was that he was headed for a thrashing by the GOP. First-term presidents almost always suffered shellackings in the midterm elections. In 1994, during Bill Clinton's first term, the Democrats lost 52 seats in the House and 8 in the Senate. In 2010, on Barack Obama's watch, the party lost 63 and 6, respectively. Political pundits were almost unanimously predicting a "red wave" that would swamp the Democrats.

And yet, on the evening of November 8, 2022, the Democrats turned those predictions on their heads. Despite persistent inflation and his low approval rating, Biden and the Democrats defied expectations by suffering minimal losses in the House and *gaining* a seat in the Senate. It was the strongest midterm performance by a first-term president in decades.

Before the elections, Biden had been criticized for harping on MAGA's assault on democracy and the threat to women's reproductive rights. And yet exit polls showed that concern for democracy and a backlash against the Dobbs decision had been decisive issues for Democrats.

Moreover, Election Day had been a thorough repudiation of candidates endorsed by Trump. It was true that J.D. Vance, a Never-Trumper-turned-MAGA acolyte, had won a Senate seat in Ohio. But most Trump disciples in competitive races were crushed. Nationwide, ten election-denying candidates for governor were defeated.

A week later, on November 15, 2022, in the ballroom at Mar-a-Lago, Donald Trump formally announced that he was running for president of the United States. It was a subdued, joyless affair, attended by a smattering of wealthy Palm Beach friends and a small band of press corps. Trump gave a long speech that was meandering and uninspiring. He looked bored.

In attendance were Trump's son Eric and son-in-law Jared Kushner—but not Ivanka. She was at the couple's new home in Miami, a $24 million waterfront mansion on Indian Creek Island. She posted a message on Instagram. "I love my father very much," she wrote. "This time around, I am choosing to prioritize my young children and the private life we are creating as a family. I do not plan to be involved in politics."

The major networks declined to carry Trump's speech, and even Fox News cut away to conservative host Laura Ingraham's show before he'd finished. Meanwhile there was a lot of talk about the possible presidential candidacy of the newly reelected governor DeSantis.

BY THE SPRING OF 2023, JOE BIDEN'S GRIP ON THE DEMOCRATIC nomination appeared secure. He was buoyed by the Democrats' surprisingly strong showing in the midterms. In February, the Democratic National Committee had endorsed Biden's re-election and decreed that there would be no primary debates. So far, his only challenger for the nomination was Marianne Williamson, the eccentric, self-help author. Then, on April 19, in Boston, where his uncle Ted had challenged Jimmy Carter back in 1980, Robert F. Kennedy, Jr., announced that he was running for the Democratic nomination for president.

On April 25, 2023, in a video emphasizing "freedom," Joe Biden formally announced his reelection bid. He appeared to be gliding toward the nomination. Yet some dissenting voices could be heard. They were muted at first, but a drumbeat for a nomi-nee other than Biden was growing. It came from political writers and analysts, including the author Jonathan Alter, Mark Leibo-vich of *The Atlantic*, Gail Collins of *The New York Times*, and Mark McKinnon of *Vanity Fair*.

Leibovich wrote, "There has to be one good Challenger X out there from the party's supposed 'deep bench,' right? Some-one who is compelling, formidable, and younger than, say, 65." That person, he argued, should "make a refreshing nuisance of themselves" and fight Biden for the nomination.

Yet no one other than Williamson and Kennedy had come forward. And no one was taking them seriously. The party con-sensus was that Biden was well on his way to winning more than enough delegates to clinch the nomination. There was no feasible Plan B. Writing for *Vanity Fair*, I confidently predicted that Biden would head the Democratic ticket.

Bill Daley, son of the legendary 1960s Democratic kingmaker, Chicago mayor Richard Daley, thought the situation was crazy. How could the party overlook Biden's dismal approval rating? "The public hasn't been with him since the very brief period from the inauguration to the Afghanistan withdrawal," he said. "At that point his approval rating was over fifty. But then it collapsed and never went up again. And the internal polling only got worse."

But Democratic success in the midterms seemed to freeze Biden's potential rivals in place. And no one in the party dared talk about his obvious vulnerability: his age. "Everyone ignored it," said Daley. "And every politician, every big shot, they all bought into the attitude that if you run against him and he gets softened up and loses to Trump, you'll be blamed and your career is over. Every freaking one of them had no balls."

Perhaps—but bucking an incumbent president is no small thing. Eugene McCarthy and Ted Kennedy discovered this during their ill-fated challenges to Lyndon Johnson in 1968 and Jimmy Carter in 1980. And unlike LBJ and Carter, Biden hadn't been weakened by a party revolt over the Vietnam War or an Iranian hostage crisis. Jennifer Ridder, a veteran campaign operative from Biden's 2020 race, told me, "I think it would have just been hard to run and raise money against [someone] who was doing well as president. So to run a campaign against the incumbent president purely as a character attack on his intelligence, I just think would have been really challenging."

On April 26, 2023—the day after Biden's video announcement—I paid a visit to Biden's White House chief of staff, Jeff Zients. Over lunch in his West Wing office, I asked him if the president had ever talked about *not* running for reelection. He replied: "I think his fundamental calculus is that he's made real progress. There's a lot more work to do."

That was a dodge, of course. There's always more work to do; that didn't explain why only Joe Biden was qualified to do it.

On my way out of the White House, I visited with one of Biden's senior advisers. I asked him if he could imagine *any* circumstances in which the president would step away from the ticket. "What would be interesting," this adviser said, "is if he could snap his fingers and have someone of his choice as president—would he snap his fingers or not?"

The implication was that if Biden could choose his successor as the party's nominee, without the messiness of an intraparty fight, he might do so.

A few months later, in July of 2023, I attended a small dinner party in Water Mill, Long Island. Among the guests were Carl Bernstein, 79, who'd broken the Watergate scandal for *The Washington Post*, and Robert Caro, 87, author of the acclaimed five-part biography of Lyndon Johnson. (Caro was still writing the fifth volume, covering LBJ and the Vietnam War.) The dinner host asked us to predict who the 2024 Democratic nominee would be.

Caro got the last word. "I think the day will come," he said, "when the party's leaders will approach Joe Biden—the way Barry Goldwater and his colleagues approached Richard Nixon in 1974. And they will say, 'Mr. President, for the good of the party and the country, we believe you should step aside.'"

4

"HOW ARE THEY LETTING THIS THING GO ON?"

Ron DeSantis was so excited he could barely contain himself. It was November 8, 2022, and the governor of Florida was bobbing like a marionette on a Tampa stage bedecked with a giant American flag. An ambitious, onetime Trump acolyte, DeSantis, 44, had just been reelected, crushing former Democratic governor Charlie Crist, 59 to 40 percent. Chopping the air with his hand, DeSantis, the self-declared warrior against "woke" culture, declared, "We not only won the election, we have rewritten the political map!" The map DeSantis had in mind stretched from sea to shining sea. As *Politico* put it, DeSantis's election night event "was designed less for a reelection party and more as a preview of what's to come: a 2024 presidential run."

In a GOP that was supposedly sick and tired of Donald Trump, DeSantis was briefly its next great hope. He was touted as Trump without the baggage—an electable, hard-right conservative without the vendettas, the angry tweets, the felonies, or the attempted insurrection. The day after DeSantis's election to a second term as governor, November 9, 2022, the *New York Post*'s front page featured the governor with his wife, Casey, and their toddlers in front of an enormous American flag, with the headline "DeFUTURE."

Seven months later, on May 24, 2023, DeSantis announced his long-anticipated campaign for the presidency. He launched it not at a public rally but on Twitter—in an audio-only chat with Elon Musk, the eccentric right-wing billionaire who'd recently acquired the social media website. The trouble began immediately. Technical difficulties caused the site to crash for the first twenty-five minutes. DeSantis was roundly mocked. "Wow! The DeSanctus TWITTER launch is a DISASTER!," Trump posted on his site, Truth Social. "His whole campaign will be a disaster. WATCH!" Biden's campaign piled on; it posted a fundraising link on Twitter—with the message "This link works."

But technical issues aside, by the time of his May announcement, DeSantis's star was already fading. His approval rating, once within striking distance of Trump, had plummeted; an ABC News 7 poll put the former president ahead of the Florida governor, 51 to 25 percent. Attempting to win over MAGA followers, DeSantis had made a hard-right turn—enacting a six-week abortion ban, banning books, and picking a fight with the state's biggest employer, Disney, over its opposition to a "Don't Say Gay" bill for Florida's schools. His extreme agenda seemed to backfire. Initially intrigued with DeSantis, many deep-pocketed donors started to have second thoughts.

Still, DeSantis was considered the only realistic challenger to Trump for the GOP nomination. Other, less serious contenders included the former U.S. ambassador to the U.N., Nikki Haley, biotech entrepreneur Vivek Ramaswamy, former vice president Mike Pence, and ex–New Jersey governor Chris Christie. All of them, it turned out, were on a fool's errand in a party that still belonged to Trump.

DeSantis's futile primary campaign lasted just eight months. Despite his political strength in Florida, he was a dismal candidate on the national stage. The opposite of an instinctive, charismatic politician, DeSantis was a bumbler who seemed unable to put a foot right. On the campaign trail he was awkward, hamhanded, and looked as if he'd rather be anywhere else. Wearing white boots while inspecting hurricane damage, he became a national laughingstock. More important, voters just thought he was phony. DeSantis portrayed himself as Trump without the attitude. But in a MAGA-dominated party where the genuine item was still available, few voters were looking for Trump Lite.

The end came at the Iowa Caucus on January 15, 2024. DeSantis had visited all ninety-nine of Iowa's counties to no avail. His well-funded super PAC, Never Back Down, was touted as a formidable turnout and canvassing machine and DeSantis earned key endorsements. But he lost to Trump by 30 percentage points and barely edged Haley for second place. Six days later, on January 21, DeSantis withdrew from the race and endorsed Trump.

BY EARLY 2024, AS JOE BIDEN'S CAMPAIGN GATHERED STEAM, his aides had become defensive and peevish. Anyone who questioned Biden's viability for reelection was a target. When David Axelrod tweeted that he doubted Biden's bid for reelection was in "HIS best interest or the country's," Ron Klain, Biden's former White House chief of staff, shot back: "Man who called Biden 'Mr. Magoo' in Aug 2019 is still at it." Even the president joined in the frat-boy insult-fest, reportedly calling Axelrod "a prick" behind closed doors.

This churlishness extended to the administration's dealings with the press. From the beginning, Anita Dunn regarded the media as a hostile adversary. This us-versus-them mentality was personified by TJ Ducklo, a White House deputy press secretary and Dunn disciple. Ducklo, 35, had been fired during Biden's first year for threatening to "destroy" a reporter who was writing a story that touched on Ducklo's personal life. But three years later, in February 2024, Dunn's attack dog was back, working for the campaign, bullying reporters to toe the Biden line. His counterpart at the White House was Andrew Bates, another Dunn protégé who berated reporters who dared to raise the issue of Biden's age. Alex Thompson, an Axios reporter, explained: "The White House's response every single time that it's come up for three-and-a-half years has been to deflect, to gaslight, to not tell the truth, not just to reporters, not just to other Democrats, but even at times to themselves."

In contrast to Dunn's aggressive acolytes, Jen Psaki, the administration's first White House press secretary, was a refreshingly honest broker—her closeness to Biden, like press secretary Jody Powell's kinship with Jimmy Carter, allowed her to speak her mind.

Biden's campaign was not only thin skinned but tin eared. Dunn's efforts to showcase the president's achievements were opaque. As a former White House official pointed out, "She was the architect of the 'Build Back Better' branding—which in the end failed and was an embarrassment."

"Build Back Better" was the clunky title of an ambitious Biden bill that stalled in Congress—which included infrastructure, universal preschool, homecare for the elderly, and paid family and medical leave, among other things. On Dunn's watch, Biden's economic successes were sold as "Bidenomics"—which to many Americans became synonymous not with jobs created and unemployment reduced (which both happened dramatically under Biden) but with inflation rising.

In Dunn's view, every press request was a landmine. For example, in early February, CBS offered Biden a Super Bowl interview, traditionally a light, softball affair that would air to an audience of millions right before the game, on February 11. Instead of an opportunity, Dunn saw a trap. She declined the offer (for the second straight year), saying the venue was inappropriate. "We hope viewers enjoy watching what they tuned in for—the game," said Ben LaBolt, the White House spokesperson. But in fact, Dunn's team feared the interview would focus on an about-to-be-released report by Special Counsel Robert Hur. The 388-page investigation of the president's handling of classified documents, released on February 5, called Biden a "well-meaning, elderly man with a poor memory."

When I asked a White House aide about this months later, he replied, "Did we want to have a 15-minute Super Bowl interview about the Hur report? The answer was no." Of course, Biden could have defused the report by answering a few questions about it with his trademark sense of humor. Instead, the president ducked a chance to show millions of viewers that he was still up to the job.

No wonder Biden got little credit for his considerable first-term achievements. He'd pulled the economy out of a nosedive, created more jobs than any other first-term president, and passed a raft of bipartisan legislation. Yet despite his dismal approval rating, the president was in a strong position politically. His only challenger for the nomination, Dean Phillips, an obscure congressman from Minnesota, never found a compelling message and ended up winning a total of four delegates. On January 23, despite not being on the ballot, Biden won the New Hampshire primary in a landslide with write-in votes. On March 12, in the Georgia primary, Biden crossed the threshold of 1,975 delegates, clinching the nomination.

Meanwhile, Biden's campaign was building a formidable infrastructure. Julie Chávez Rodriguez, granddaughter of the legendary labor leader Cesar Chávez, was the nominal campaign manager. But the race was being run out of the White House by a troika: Jen O'Malley Dillon, Mike Donilon, and Dunn. In January, O'Malley Dillon and Donilon officially decamped from the White House to the campaign headquarters in Wilmington, Delaware (though Donilon hopped back and forth). O'Malley Dillon took control of the campaign's ground game. Donilon was in charge of messaging, which included multimillion-dollar ad buys aimed at building up the president and tearing down Trump.

In March of 2024, Biden's advisers hatched a bold idea: Challenge Trump to two debates—and schedule the first in June. That would be the earliest presidential debate in modern history. "The overwhelming strategic thinking," said a senior adviser, "was that we needed to force this thing more into a choice as opposed to a referendum." Indeed, the race had become a referendum on an aging incumbent whose record on the economy was unpopular. Voters had not yet grasped that the only alternative to Biden was Trump. An early debate could reframe the campaign as a clear choice between the two men.

There was another factor in the Biden camp's decision—one that would prove ironic. As another campaign aide put it: "An early debate would quiet fears that the president was infirm." In any event, it promised to be pivotal. Months before the early debate was proposed, a prominent former Democratic campaign manager told me that a Biden-Trump debate would be crucial in the 2024 election. That was because, as he put it, "people really wanted to know two things: Does Biden still have it? And is Trump still a whack job?"

The outcome would depend on which Biden showed up: the energetic speaker who outwitted right-wing GOP hecklers at the 2024 State of the Union address or the frail octogenarian who struggled to complete sentences. Biden's advisers were gambling on the former. O'Malley Dillon pitched the June debate proposal to CNN. On May 15, the network accepted, proposing a presidential debate on June 27. That same day, both campaigns agreed to the event—and to a second face-off in September, to air on ABC.

IN THE SPRING OF 2024, WORD BEGAN TO SPREAD OF A SURPRISing new addition to Trump's campaign team: Paul Manafort. Even for Trump, embracing his disgraced, ex–campaign chairman seemed brazen. I asked a well-known former GOP political strategist what he made of it. "It means that crooks like crooks and grifters like grifters," he said.

Manafort and I connected almost accidentally. In March of 2024, I'd been interviewing a veteran GOP campaign operative, who emailed me afterward: "Did I mention that I'm staying at Paul Manafort's house?" He had not. I took him up on his offer to introduce us by Zoom. Until recently, Manafort's home had been a prison cell at the Loretto Federal Correctional Institution in central Pennsylvania. After being imprisoned for nearly two years, Manafort had been released to home confinement at his house in Palm Gardens, Florida. His lawyers argued that because he suffered from high blood pressure, liver disease, and respiratory ailments, he was at risk of dying from COVID.

But now Manafort was a free man. On December 23, 2020, Trump had granted him a pardon for all the crimes he'd committed—including witness tampering, obstruction, money laundering, tax fraud, and perjury.

Manafort, 75, spoke to me from the living room of his home, a twenty-minute drive from Mar-a-Lago; a housekeeper scurried about in the background. He appeared tanned and relaxed—and, except for a mane of white hair, not a day older than he was when he strode into Trump Tower in 2016. It was as though he'd never been accused of controlling an illegal, multimillion-dollar Ukrainian "black ledger"; been labeled a grave national security threat for sharing internal polling data with an alleged Russian spy; been ignominiously fired by Jared Kushner over breakfast; and been convicted and sentenced to more than seven years in prison. Manafort was clearly enjoying his newfound good fortune. He was back in the game, on top of the world.

I wasn't yet ready to ask Manafort about the story Reagan's ex–campaign manager Ed Rollins told me—the one about that suitcase stuffed with $10 million. We'd get around to that later.

I WANTED TO KNOW WHAT MANAFORT THOUGHT ABOUT THE AP-proaching presidential debate. Some political observers believed the Biden campaign had set a trap and Trump had walked into it. After all, CNN was considered a Biden-friendly network and O'Malley Dillon had negotiated the ground rules: There would be no live audience and the mics of the candidates would be muted when they weren't speaking.

Manafort swatted away this argument. "They thought they

snookered us on getting CNN," he said. "But frankly, that was an opportunity that fell in our lap. CNN doing the first debate is actually perfect for us because it's the audience we're targeting and we'll have our messages very honed in on those people for that debate."

There was no risk for Trump in a debate, Manafort insisted—because he already had an insurmountable lead in the swing states. "You look at the internal polls on all of the issues for the election: inflation, the economy, border, law and order, foreign policy," he said. "These are the top issues. And Trump is either at significant double digit or eight or nine points ahead of Biden. And not just with Republicans."

According to Manafort, asking for the early debate was a desperate ploy by Biden's people. "They need to change the dynamic because if they don't, the race is over in June," he said. "And so that's why they want a June debate—that's a Hail Mary pass. It's all risk for Biden. And it's all plus for us."

To Manafort, everything about the 2024 campaign reminded him of the glory days of the 2016 race. "I remember one time we were pulling out of Trump Tower to go catch a plane to an event," he recalled. "And we had a four-to-five-car motorcade. And he's looking at this motorcade. I say, 'It'll be a lot different when you're president.' And he says, 'You know, that's what I was just thinking. This is going to be my life now.'" Trump was sure he would win, Manafort said. "I believe he never thought he would lose."

Those "hunger and swagger" days were long gone. Now Trump had a well-oiled, battle-tested team of professionals led by Wiles and LaCivita. They had pollsters and data crunchers and social media influencers and opposition researchers—and plenty of money (much of it raised from small donors in response to Trump's indictments and convictions). Trump's campaign had taken over the Republican National Committee and staffed it with Trump family and loyalists, making daughter-in-law Lara Trump co-chair and LaCivita chief operating officer. Wiles and LaCivita had helped Trump destroy Florida governor Ron De-Santis, former U.N. ambassador Nikki Haley, and all other rivals for the GOP nomination. But could they pull off another 2016 miracle?

Recently news had broken of a controversial addition to the Trump campaign: Corey Lewandowski, Trump's 2016 campaign manager, was a fixture on the Trump campaign plane. I asked Manafort by text what he made of that. "The guy is a thug," he replied. On a Zoom call, I pressed Manafort about his old nemesis. "He *begged* Trump to let him come back on the campaign, literally begged him," Manafort said.

When I reached Lewandowski by phone about a month later, to get his side of the story, he replied: "Why would I beg for a free job?" Trump's former campaign manager said he was getting no salary. "Did Trump ask you to come back?" I asked him. "He did," Lewandowski said. "That's the only reason I'm here." Lewandowski said he'd made sixty-five campaign television appearances the previous week. "My only interest is seeing Trump win," he said.

I asked Lewandowski if he'd bumped into Manafort. "Not once," he said—and then added, "Although I don't hang around with a lot of felons. I don't know if he's still technically a felon." (Manafort is a felon. A pardon does not expunge a criminal record.) I didn't point out to Lewandowski that his constant companion Trump was also a felon, thirty-four times over.

The 2024 Trump campaign was a hothouse of internecine intrigue and backstabbing. Not only were Manafort and Lewandowski enemies, but Wiles and LaCivita were badmouthing Lewandowski. They didn't dare throw him off the campaign plane because Trump wanted him around. But the co–campaign managers not only resented Lewandowski's closeness to Trump, they thought he was spying on them.

And they were right. Lewandowski had done an audit of the 2024 campaign's spending at Trump's request. On the record, Lewandowski wouldn't tell me if this was true but agreed that he'd be the perfect guy for the job—since "unlike Paul Manafort or all these other guys, no one's ever accused Corey Lewandowski of stealing a dime ever in his life."

In this case the alleged culprit was not Manafort but LaCivita. Lewandowski believed LaCivita was less interested in electing Trump than in making a killing. Trump's former campaign manager thought LaCivita was exploiting the former president by spending a fortune on multimillion-dollar ad buys and pocketing a percentage of the budget. "The only way you can make money is if you spend the money," said Lewandowski. "The vested interest is to spend the money, not to win the election."

That wasn't illegal, but it was the kind of thing that could send Trump into a rage. A few months after I spoke with Lewandowski about this, journalist Michael Isikoff reported in *The Daily Beast,* on October 15, 2024, that LaCivita had been paid at least $22 million for his services to the Trump campaign. Isikoff later revised this figure to $19.2 million.

Wiles and LaCivita's grip on the campaign suddenly seemed threatened. Would Trump blow his stack and fire them before Election Day? Lewandowski doubted it: "Do you deal with this problem post-election?" he asked rhetorically. "Sure. Why not? Because if you win, nobody cares. Right? And if you lose, there's only two people getting the blame." That would be Wiles and LaCivita, of course.

In the meantime, Lewandowski and Manafort were giving each other a wide berth. And Manafort was trying to stay out of the press—but not very successfully. On May 10, 2024, *The Washington Post* reported that Manafort had been "assisting an effort to launch a Netflix-like mobile streaming and entertainment platform in China." The paper noted that he was making "introductions for individuals seeking to do business with an increasingly assertive China, at the very moment that Trump's GOP is presenting itself as a foe of the ruling Chinese Communist Party."

Manafort insisted this was "a total bogus thing." He had only made "introductions to a couple of studios," and had "nothing to do with China, including Chinese businesses, government, individuals, or anything else." But the next day he announced he was resigning from the Trump campaign: "I called Wiles and said, 'Susie, look, I'll do everything you need me to do. Donald's not going to want this.'"

But Manafort's "resignation" was just for public consumption; he'd keep working for the campaign under the radar.

Manafort was helping to plan the 2024 GOP convention, which was set to begin in Milwaukee, Wisconsin, on July 15. He'd blocked out themes for the four-day event: Monday: Make America Wealthy Once Again (the economy). Tuesday: Make America Safe Once Again (crime). Wednesday: Make America Strong Once Again (national security). And Thursday: Make America Great Once Again (Trump's acceptance speech).

But the Trump campaign was looking beyond the convention. Eight years before, they'd been unprepared to govern. "That's going to be very different this year," Manafort told me, "because he's got a whole team now. And these are people who are pro-Trump's agenda. And they are doing work that will be part of a transition."

"Is this the Project 2025 people?" I asked.

"Right," he replied.

Project 2025, of course, was the infamous blueprint for a second Trump presidential term. A team of right-wing ideologues, including former Trump officials, had been laboring over it for months. The result was a strikingly fascistic-sounding document, detailing how a second Trump administration would put flesh on the bones of his authoritarian agenda.

It was a hefty, 922-page tome; indeed, at the Democratic Convention in Chicago that summer, Kenan Thompson of *Saturday Night Live* would quip, "It could kill a small animal and democracy at the same time." Project 2025 had something for every would-be strongman: stiff federal restrictions on abortion; detention camps for undocumented immigrants; replacing civil servants and objective experts in federal agencies with MAGA lackeys. And the list went on.

It was a manual for uprooting the Deep State that Trump had railed against—that shadowy cabal of liberals dedicated to stopping him at every turn. Never mind that this cabal was a figment of Trump's imagination.

Project 2025 was so extreme, it was politically radioactive. That's why Trump repeatedly denied knowing anything about the project. "I have no idea who is behind it," he said. But Manafort was less reticent. "They're doing the work now," he told me excitedly. "This didn't exist in 2017."

If all this planning for a second term seemed like measuring the drapes for the Oval Office before they'd moved in, Trump's advisers were unabashed. Indeed, all the flattering media coverage seemed to be going to Wiles's and LaCivita's heads. In an interview with the writer Tim Alberta, LaCivita predicted a 320-electoral-vote Trump landslide. And when Alberta asked the co–campaign managers if electoral college blowouts were a thing of the past:

> *They exchanged glances.*
> *"You know, I could make a case—" Wiles began.*
> *"I could too," LaCivita said. He was grinning.*

But they had reason to be cocky: They thought Trump would be running against Joe Biden.

IN THE SPRING OF 2024, BIDEN WAS LOOKING FORWARD TO HIS reelection race. But there were plenty of warning signs that the president wasn't up to it. In March, a veteran Democratic operative interviewed for a top campaign job with Biden and his aides in the Oval Office. "I was like, what is happening here?" she recalled. "He wasn't asking questions. It was everyone else, not him. And it felt like they were just trying to cover up that he didn't really know what was going on." The job interview took a surprisingly frank turn. "Part of their discussion on the strategy of the campaign was 'Hey, in 2020 we had this great excuse of the basement, of COVID, to keep him out of the public eye. We no longer have that excuse. What do we do?' They were saying, 'He doesn't have the energy. He can't go on the campaign trail all the time. How do we fix that?'"

Over Saint Patrick's Day weekend, at a small White House party, Biden spoke to guests using a teleprompter. Bill Daley, who was there, couldn't believe it. If the president needed a script for a small gathering of Irish guys, how would he survive the rigors of a campaign? "How are they letting this thing go on?" he thought. "This is crazy."

Biden's deterioration was something you couldn't un-see—and yet his closest aides seemed to be doing just that. I asked Daley, "How were they not seeing what you saw, what others saw?" When you work for the president, he replied, "you're in the bubble. You've crossed the Rubicon." Once you'd suspended disbelief, there was no turning back. "Everybody bought into it," said Daley. "And once they crossed the Rubicon, they bullshitted everybody to stay out of the race."

At that Saint Patrick's Day party at the White House, Daley ran into his friend Tom Donilon, a veteran national security expert and brother of Biden's adviser Mike. They talked about the elephant in the room. Why hadn't anyone spoken to the president about stepping aside and giving someone else a chance to beat Trump? "How are they letting this fucking thing go on?" Daley asked him. Donilon shook his head. "I don't believe there's anyone who's had the conversation with him about not running, including my brother," he said. If Mike Donilon, Biden's alter ego, hadn't spoken to the president about his age, it was almost certain that no one had.

In May, Daley went to a fundraiser for the president's re-election campaign in a Chicago apartment with about forty guests. "I'll tell you, I got rattled," he said. "They had a receiving line, a photo line. And I had not seen the president up close in a couple of years. And I went through it with my wife—and he was friendly and all that, but he was just not the same guy."

When Daley heard that Biden's aides were considering a June debate, he was aghast. It was pure hubris. "They were so cocky," he said. "They got CNN, they got the moderators, they got the rules—no audience. They were telling everyone: 'We got everything we wanted.'" But Daley foresaw disaster. Meanwhile, the president's friends and allies seemed delusional. "They would say, 'Oh, Joe, he can do it. Don't hold him back. Let Joe be Joe.' One of the president's best friends gave me this one day—'They're holding him back!' I told him, They weren't holding him back. They knew he couldn't do it!"

Yet now they were sending Biden onto the field against Trump, with the election on the line, in a nationally televised debate. It made no sense to Daley. He called up Biden's chief of staff, Jeff Zients. "Jeff, I know you're debating whether to debate," he told him. "Do not do this. I'm telling you, don't do it. I'm just telling you, come up with something, but do not do it."

NANCY D'ALESANDRO PELOSI WAS A TOWERING FIGURE ON Capitol Hill and in the Democratic Party. A congresswoman representing California's 11th district since 1987, she was a two-time Speaker of the House of Representatives (from 2007 to 2011 and 2019 to 2023). She'd been instrumental in steering Barack Obama's landmark Affordable Care Act (ACA) through Congress. And she'd stood up not only to President Trump in the Oval Office but to the violent mob that had rampaged through the Capitol on January 6, 2021. She was, as Ezra Klein of *The New York Times* put it, "one of the last people left in politics who knows how to wield power and why she wants to do so."

For months Pelosi had watched with concern as Joe Biden's shrinking poll numbers threatened to sink not only his reelection but that of down-ballot Democrats as well. She'd fielded calls from alarmed Democratic donors and panicked members of her caucus alike. (Though Pelosi was Speaker Emerita, she still considered it *her* caucus.) The president's dwindling prospects pained her because she and Biden were good friends; they often talked about American history and swapped stories about their grandchildren.

Pelosi believed Biden's advisers were misleading him, showing him rosy poll numbers. She'd never been impressed by them; in her mind, they were an old boys' club who talked only to themselves.

In early May, Pelosi went to the White House to accept the nation's highest civilian award: the Presidential Medal of Freedom. Seated on a stage festooned with American flags in the East Room, she was startled by how much the president had aged. "He was not the same Joe Biden," she later told a friend.

Yet the president muddled through. Flanked by other medal recipients, Pelosi listened as Biden showered her with praise. "Nancy is a brilliant, practical, principled, and determined leader," he said. "Her accomplishments are overwhelming. And I predict," the president said, glancing proudly at his friend, "and I've said this to her for a while: History will remember you, Nancy, as the greatest speaker of the House of Representatives ever." Applause filled the room. When it subsided, Biden said, "We've had some great speakers, Nancy, but I love you, kid. I really do love you."

As the president draped the medal around her neck, Pelosi stared straight ahead. Then she turned and gave Biden a perfunctory peck on the cheek and headed for her chair.

It should have been a glorious moment, a celebration. But for Pelosi, it was awkward, even painful. Medals were nice. But winning the House and Senate and retaining the White House were more important. She couldn't shake the realization that Joe Biden was a shadow of himself.

5

"WE HAD A LONG TALK ABOUT AMERICA."

On Friday, June 21, 2024, Joe Biden arrived at Camp David to prepare for the most important test of his presidency. The televised CNN presidential debate with Donald Trump, just six days away, might well decide the outcome of the 2024 election.

Preparing for a modern presidential debate is a massive and elaborate undertaking. (At least it is for Democrats; Trump's preparation consisted mostly of spitballing with a few aides.) In Biden's case, the process had begun months earlier. A replica of CNN's studio had been constructed inside a helicopter hangar at Camp David, where the set was meticulously re-created down to the cameras, lighting, and acoustics. Stand-ins were recruited for the mock debates: Biden's lawyer Bob Bauer played Trump; Anita Dunn and Ben LaBolt, a communications aide, played CNN moderators Dana Bash and Jake Tapper, respectively. Videotape of the anchors' previous debate performances was scrutinized in an effort to predict which questions Biden would be asked.

Producing a presidential debate prep was almost like directing a Hollywood movie. In this case, literally. Before leaving his home in Wilmington, Delaware, for Camp David, the president sat down for a Zoom call with Steven Spielberg and Jeffrey Katzenberg. The famous director and producer coached the president on his body language, directing him not only on how to deliver his lines but how to present himself in cutaways when Trump was speaking.

Spielberg had coached Biden before his 2024 State of the Union address—an experience that impressed Bruce Reed, his deputy chief of staff. "You can see watching him what a great coach he is on what to emphasize, how to pace yourself," said Reed. "He just knows how to bring out the best in somebody."

With Spielberg's help, Biden brought his best to the State of the Union, dominating his GOP hecklers and owning the occasion. But debates are different from speeches; the president would have less control—and he was playing opposite the ultimate scene stealer, Donald Trump.

At his first meeting with Biden in Aspen Lodge, the president's cabin, Ron Klain was startled. He'd never seen him so exhausted and out of it. Biden was unaware of what was happening in his own campaign. Halfway through the session, the president excused himself and went off to sit by the pool.

That evening Biden met again with Klain and his team, Mike Donilon, Steve Ricchetti, and Bruce Reed. "We sat around the table," said Klain. "He had answers on cards, and he was just extremely exhausted. And I was struck by how out of touch with American politics he was. He was just very, very focused on his interactions with NATO leaders."

It was a Joe Biden whom Klain barely recognized. During his first two years in office, when Klain was his White House chief of staff, Biden had been deeply engaged in domestic affairs and proud of his legislative record. Now he was obsessed with foreign leaders and what they thought of him. This fixation had begun, Klain thought, on October 7, 2023, when Hamas launched its vicious attack on Israel, killing more than 1,200 men, women, and children. Since then, Biden had lost interest in domestic affairs. He reminded Klain of George H.W. Bush during the waning days of his one-term presidency, when the commander of the Gulf War seemed intent on taking a victory lap and had little interest in the economy.

Klain wondered half-seriously if Biden thought he was president of NATO instead of the U.S. "He just became very enraptured with being the head of NATO," he said. That wouldn't help him on Capitol Hill because, as Klain noted, "domestic political leaders don't really care what Macron and Scholz think."

On Monday morning, June 24, Biden felt terrible and his voice was weak. Gathered in the hangar-turned-CNN studio were Klain, Ricchetti, Donilon, Reed, Dunn, and Bauer—and Katzenberg, who'd flown in for the week. The Hollywood mogul and self-described "super-triple-type A" personality had studied videotape of Biden's previous debates and coached him on how to improve his "physicality." Others came and went during the week, including Brian Deese, former director of Biden's National Economic Council; Jake Sullivan, national security adviser; and Jeff Zients, White House chief of staff.

Klain tried to get the president to talk about domestic affairs in two mock debates. The first was scheduled to last ninety minutes but Klain called it off after forty-five. The president's voice was shot and so was his grasp of the subject. "All he really could talk about was his infrastructure plan and how he was rebuilding America and sixteen million jobs," said Klain. Biden had nothing to say about his agenda for a second term.

Klain prodded him: "Look, sir, you're not really telling people what you're going to do if they reelect you."

Biden grew irritable. "I'm not going to make more promises," he snapped. "I made too many promises in 2020 and I delivered on most of them, and all people remember are the things I didn't deliver on." Klain retorted: "Well, you have to make some promises to get reelected, sir."

Klain tried to remind the president about his unfinished first-term agenda. "You ran in 2020 and we put in Build Back Better and didn't get it done, lowering childcare costs." Biden replied: "Well, how would I do that?"

"Well, you had a whole plan that passed the House of Representatives but didn't pass the Senate that would subsidize state and local efforts to do childcare and bring down the cost to twenty dollars a day. And you ought to try to fight for it again." Biden seemed befuddled. "Well, that just seems like a big spending program," he said.

"No, sir. It brings down costs for people. It's responsive to inflation. It will bring more people into the workforce. It's good economics. And you know this is something you're for."

Biden didn't want to talk about it. In hopes of piquing his interest, Klain arranged a phone call with Melinda French Gates, a persuasive childcare advocate. Biden perked up briefly but soon lost interest again.

Twenty-five minutes into the second mock debate, the president was done for the day. "I'm just too tired to continue and I'm afraid of losing my voice here and I feel bad," he said. "I just need some sleep. I'll be fine tomorrow." He went off to bed.

Klain was deeply worried. He tried to remind himself that Biden had always been a game-day player. Maybe the president would rise to the occasion as he had often done before.

AT MAR-A-LAGO, DONALD TRUMP WAS PREPARING FOR THE DE-bate in his own way. Unlike most candidates, Trump was essentially unbriefable. When he was president, he didn't even want to sit for the President's Daily Brief, given by the Department of National Intelligence; he thought he knew everything worth knowing. So Trump's debate prep sessions consisted mostly of bouncing lines off advisers. They were led by "the Millers"—Stephen, his speechwriter and hardline anti-immigration advocate, and Jason, his communications strategist.

In debates, Trump often took an undisciplined approach, overwhelming his opponents with a firehose of half-truths, calumny, and outright lies. But Paul Manafort insisted that this time, against Biden, Trump would be disciplined and focused "on the core issues, what people are worried about."

"Our challenge," he told me, in one of our frequent Zoom calls, "is to keep people focused on where they are right now, which is they think Biden's a failed president. Trump's a successful president from their personal standpoint, which is the bottom line. And he will keep saying, are you better off today than you were four years ago?"

"Our confidence in the two candidates being face-to-face is very high," he said. "Trump is on his game. They say, well, he hasn't debated in eight years. He's debating every day and dealing with his legal issues. His mind is sharp on where he needs to be."

• • •

On debate night, Biden arrived at CNN headquarters just before the 9 p.m. start time. He was offered a "walk-through"—a chance to check out the camera angles from the podium—but he waved it off. Minutes later, the president and Trump took the stage.

An hour earlier, at his hotel, Biden's voice had been fine— but now it was little more than a whisper. "The biggest surprise of the first few moments," said Reed, "was that his voice had almost disappeared. That was a complete shock." Reed found it hard to watch.

Twelve minutes later came disaster. Asked about the deficit, Biden gave the most incoherent answer ever uttered in a presidential debate. It ended with "We finally beat Medicare."

The president froze, his expression vacant; he seemed unaware of where he was. Some observers wondered if he was having a ministroke.

From behind the stage, in a green room, Chris LaCivita looked at Susie Wiles and Tony Fabrizio, their pollster, and said: "He's dead. He's not going to stay."

Ron Klain thought he recognized what was happening to Biden.

"One, he wasn't dialed in," he said. "Two, he was exhausted and sick. And three, his stutter is a bit of an auditory processing thing. He's always had a problem reacting quickly to what people say to him. In that moment, it definitely got the best of him. And that's what froze him up, it was him trying to figure out what to say." Biden's declaration, "We finally beat Medicare," was a case of transposing two thoughts. What he meant to say was "We finally beat Big Pharma." His wires were crossed.

Bruce Reed offered his own diagnosis. "When you've grown up learning to overcome a stutter, the most important thing is to keep talking. If you slow down or stop, you're afraid you're not going to be able to start again." Reed compared it to down-hill skiing. "It's beautiful to watch unless you pick up too much speed or there's a sudden mogul or branch that wasn't there before. And when that happens, things can go wrong. That's what happened in that answer."

As the debate wore on, Biden continued to career off the slope. Trump recognized what was happening and let his opponent wipe out. At one point, after an incomprehensible jumble of words from Biden, Trump parried: "I really don't know what he said at the end of that sentence and I don't think he knows what he said, either."

It was the truest thing Trump had ever said in a debate.

At a "debate watch party" for high-roller Democratic donors in downtown Atlanta, the mood was somber. After Biden's "Medicare" gaffe, everyone's cell phones went off simultaneously. Many if not most of the donors were thinking the same thing about the president's candidacy: "It's over." As they took phone calls from frantic donors, a Latina stood off to the side by herself. It was Julie Chávez Rodriguez, Biden's campaign manager.

Klain, Donilon, Ricchetti, Sullivan, and Annie Tomasini were watching the debate from a room below the CNN stage. On a Zoom monitor they could see Jen O'Malley Dillon, Reed, and a few campaign staffers; they were at a separate location, monitoring "dial groups"—focus groups of voters who turned a dial up or down to register their approval or disapproval in real time. The Biden dials were headed south. "We knew we were in trouble," said an aide.

It was the understatement of the campaign. Whatever the cause of Biden's difficulties that night, it was the most disastrous performance ever delivered in a presidential debate—and a fatal blow to his hopes for reelection. By the twelve-minute mark, any objective viewer could see that the president was incapable of waging an effective campaign against Donald Trump.

But Biden's team didn't see it that way. They were in denial. Steve Ricchetti thought the president had just had a bad night—like Barack Obama's lackluster first debate against Mitt Romney in 2012. Dunn was Biden's fiercest defender. She argued that the president had actually won the debate with people who mattered. Like O'Malley Dillon, she'd been watching voter dial groups during the debate and noted that as it wore on, they'd disliked Trump even more than Biden. "It's a good illustration of the difference between voters and elites," she said. "Voters experience this differently. They hated Donald Trump. We actually picked up a few votes in the group. So it was a bad debate but it didn't feel catastrophic at all."

Biden's advisers were among the best and the brightest, adept at managing policy, politics, and public relations at the highest level. But in the wake of the debate, they were the blind leading the blind. They'd spent years, even decades, rallying around Biden whenever he came under attack; their instinct was to adopt a defensive crouch.

Bill Daley attributed this group think to being inside a bubble. Jack Watson, Jimmy Carter's former White House chief of staff, compared it to being inside a magnetic force field. The gravitational pull to protect the president was immense. Nearly four months later, when I spoke with Reed and Ricchetti at the White House, they were still stuck in that force field. The problem, they insisted, wasn't Biden's infirmity, it was three weeks of Democratic infighting and the media's obsession with his debate performance.

Watching the debate with his wife at home, Jeff Zients was

more clear-eyed. "I do what I do in all these situations," he said. "Just take a breath. It's going to be okay. Don't overreact. Start thinking through what's next. I think it was important that he got right back out there."

Biden did just that; after the debate, he and Jill flew to Raleigh, North Carolina, landing at 2 a.m. A long-planned campaign rally was scheduled for that afternoon. This was a do-or-die event; another halting, incoherent performance would surely sink Biden's candidacy.

Stepping up to the podium before a boisterous crowd, Biden looked more vigorous than he had the night before. Mike Donilon had stayed up all night writing his remarks, which rolled by on a teleprompter. Biden spoke in a loud, clear voice. "I know I'm not a young man," he cracked, "I don't debate as well as I used to, but I know what I do know: I know how to tell the truth! I know like millions of Americans know: When you get knocked down, you get back up!" The audience roared, chanting "Don't you quit!" By Biden's standards, it was an energetic, coherent performance.

For Ron Klain, the crisis was a call to arms. He knew the debate had been a disaster but believed passionately that Biden could still be the party's nominee. "President Biden had chosen a risky presidential strategy but a defensible one," he told me. "He wanted to be a president for working people and didn't do much to court the party's elite and the donor elite. And the only way that worked was with a tight alliance with the progressive wing of our party."

In Klain's view, Biden's debate fiasco opened the door to a power grab by party elites. "This was about something other than his age," Klain said. "It was a struggle over power in our party." Biden liked to boast that he was the most pro-union president ever—and had proudly walked a picket line with the United Auto Workers in Belleville, Michigan, on September 26, 2023. But the attitude of the Democratic business class, according to Klain, was "We're tired of him. He's a Big Labor guy. And we need someone who can work with the business leaders in the country."

The day after the debate, June 28, Klain called the president. "Look, we're hemorrhaging badly," he said. "We need to get the Progressive Caucus to the White House this weekend. And you need to agree with them on an agenda for a second term, and they will endorse you. So you can walk out there with one hundred members of Congress saying, 'You should stay in the race.'"

Biden wasn't convinced: "Well, I'm supposed to go to Camp David this weekend for a photo shoot with my family."

Klain was blunt: "You need to cancel that. You need to stay in Washington. You need to have an aggressive plan to fight and to rally the troops."

Biden seemed to relent. "Okay," he said.

But the president's resolve didn't last. That weekend, Biden and his family were at Camp David having their pictures taken by photographer Annie Leibovitz.

Klain was angry. He called Zients, his successor as White House chief of staff. The president needed to rally the progressives ASAP, Klain told him. But Zients didn't share his alarm. "Look, we've got a plan," he told Klain. "We've got a schedule. We're going to stick to the schedule." Zients and his team had been trying to rally Democratic support for the president, reaching out to Schumer, Jeffries, Pelosi, the Asian caucus, the Congressional Black Caucus, the Congressional Hispanic Caucus, and others. Zients had personally lobbied Vermont senator Bernie Sanders. But Klain felt more drastic action was needed.

That weekend, instead of meeting with them in person, Biden spoke with the Progressive Caucus on a Zoom call.

The conference was a fiasco. On the call were Washington state representative Pramila Jayapal and more than a dozen other members of the caucus. Instead of rallying them to his cause, Biden gave them a scolding. "All you guys want to talk about is Gaza," he snapped. "What would you have me do?" He went on: "I was a progressive before some of you guys were even in Congress."

When Klain heard about the call from Jayapal, he was furious. He called Zients again. "Hey, what the fuck happened here?" Klain demanded.

Zients replied, "Well, Steve was up there and you have to ask Steve."

Steve Richetti, Biden's head of legislative affairs and a former big business lobbyist, was the progressives' least favorite White House official. He and Mike Donilon were with the president at his Rehoboth Beach house, and Zients urged Klain to get a full read-out from Ricchetti.

Klain shot back: "Well, Steve was the wrong person for this. I told you that." Klain believed Zients didn't understand what was at stake. "Jeff, this is life or death for this presidency this weekend," he said.

Klain was admired in Biden World. He'd been an empowered White House chief with keen political instincts and was a driving force behind the president's accomplishments during his first two years. Zients, who'd made a fortune as an entrepreneur, defined the job differently. The key word in the title was "staff," as he saw it; his job was to empower others to execute the president's agenda. Klain saw himself not only as an honest broker who could tell the president hard truths but as a policy advocate.

Klain believed the president had squandered valuable time. In his view, Biden had spent a year courting Republican House Speaker Mike Johnson in search of money for Ukraine—and had dropped the ball on securing the border and other important issues. Klain was also alarmed by how much the president had been isolated from the outside world.

Zients had a different view. On his watch, the White House had brought the country out of the COVID pandemic in better shape than any other advanced economy and had defused multiple crises—the debt ceiling talks, the Silicon Valley Bank scandal, and natural disasters—that could have sunk the economy and jeopardized Biden's reelection.

Zients was unflappable; he'd succeeded in two of Washington's most difficult jobs, as Biden's coronavirus response coordinator and White House chief of staff, rarely if ever losing his composure. "Well, Ron, I believe in having people do their jobs," he told Klain. "And Steve is in charge of legislative affairs." Klain fired back: "Well, this isn't legislative affairs. This is about saving the presidency. This isn't like we're trying to get some bill passed. And you need to have a strategy to save his presidency."

For months, Democrats had been privately telling one another that Biden should step aside. But on July 2, the intraparty rebellion broke into the open. In a public statement, Texas congressman Lloyd Doggett called for Biden to end his candidacy. "I had hoped that the debate would provide some momentum" to Biden's reelection bid, he said. "Instead of reassuring voters, the president failed to effectively defend his many accomplishments and expose Trump's many lies."

Doggett was the first Democratic congressperson to call publicly for the president to withdraw.

In an effort to stanch the bleeding, on July 5, the White House accepted an interview request from ABC News's George Stephanopoulos. Biden was hoarse and semi-coherent. "I'll feel as long as I gave it my all and I did the good as job as I know I can do, that's what this is about," he said. The president had veered off the ski slope again. And he was defiant about staying in the race. "Only the Lord Almighty," Biden insisted, could persuade him to step aside.

Stephanopoulos questioned the president gently, like a grandson. Afterward, when I asked the ABC anchor by email for his impressions, he replied: "Heartbreaking up close."

Biden continued to take fire from critics. At *The New York Times*, the assault was withering. Not only the editorial board but columnists Thomas Friedman, Nicholas Kristof, and Paul Krugman called on the president to step aside. This only hardened the Biden team's bunker mentality. The president's friend Ted Kaufman was convinced that the *Times* board and its reporters, traditionally independent, were part of an anti-Biden plot. "I'll bet you a million dollars," he told me, "that they had an executive editorial board meeting and said, 'Here's what we're going to do, guys. We're all on the team.'"

Joining the Biden-must-go chorus were the creators of the podcast *Pod Save America*. Jon Favreau, Jon Lovett, and Tommy Vietor were former Obama advisers known as the "Pod Save Bros." An unnamed Biden adviser mocked them in a piece by Katie Rogers in *The New York Times*, saying they "worked for a cerebral, cool-guy president and never understood the world according to the scrappy kid from Scranton."

Lovett minced no words in his reply. "Joe Biden has been an extraordinary president," he wrote on X. "Statesman. Hero. But it's hard to deny that in the two weeks since the debate, it's the arrogant and small Joe Biden that we've seen most—hanging on, bragging, defensive, angry, weak."

Biden continued to dig in. On Monday, July 8, the White House released a letter from the president to congressional Democrats: "I want you to know that despite all the speculation in the press and elsewhere, I am firmly committed to staying in this race, to running this race to the end, and to beating Donald Trump."

The letter read like a White House press release. Nancy Pelosi would later remark, "It didn't sound like Joe Biden to me."

TWO WEEKS AFTER THE DEBATE, THE DEMOCRATIC PARTY WAS IN turmoil. Despite Biden's contentious Zoom call, the Progressive Caucus, led by Jayapal, New York congresswoman Alexandria Ocasio-Cortez, and Senator Bernie Sanders, was behind him. But moderate and conservative elected officials were rebelling—even if only a few had so far gone public. House Minority Leader Hakeem Jeffries and Senate Majority Leader Chuck Schumer feared that if Biden remained on the ticket, Democrats would suffer historic losses—surrendering not only the White House but the House and Senate as well.

Still, there was a problem with forcing the president to step aside: Biden had won more than enough delegates for the nomination, and he'd done it fair and square. A decision to drop out of the race would have to be his alone.

Moreover, pressuring him might only stiffen Biden's spine. As Katie Rogers wrote on July 10 in *The New York Times*:

> *Anger has not worked. Fear has not worked. Panic has not worked. Bluntness has not worked. Sadness has not worked.*

Concern has not worked. Elected Democrats and donors have been all over the emotional map this week.

Persuasion had not worked, either; in separate conversations with the president, both Jeffries, on the phone, and Schumer, in person, had tried to tell Biden just how dangerous it would be for him to stay in the race. And he hadn't budged.

The fact was that only one person stood a chance of persuading Biden to reconsider: Nancy Pelosi.

Pelosi had been sizing up Biden's electability for months—well before that day he awarded her the Presidential Medal of Freedom at the White House. No one was better at reading polls and counting votes and no one cared more about protecting Democrats from the MAGA threat. She was frustrated that none of the party's male power brokers—Barack Obama, Bill Clinton, Chuck Schumer, or Hakeem Jeffries—had stepped up to say something publicly.

Pelosi had only recently concluded that Biden shouldn't stay in the race. Indeed, after the Democrats' better-than-expected showing in the 2022 midterm elections, she'd privately urged the president to run for a second term. But now, in the wake of Biden's disastrous debate, she made her move.

It was time to apply pressure in public.

On July 10, Pelosi appeared on the MSNBC program *Morning Joe*, ostensibly to talk about NATO and Belarus. But the show's correspondent Jonathan Lemire steered the subject to Joe Biden: "Does he have your support to be the head of the Democratic ticket?" he asked.

Pelosi replied, "It's up to the president to decide if he is going to run. We're all encouraging him to make that decision because time is running short."

Lemire pressed her: "He has said firmly this week he is going to run. Do *you* want him to run?"

Pelosi replied, "I want him to do whatever he decides to do."

Delivered with her trademark nonchalance, the former speaker's answer was a political master stroke. She knew full well that Biden had *made* his decision—he was running. But by refusing to acknowledge that fact, Pelosi put the pressure right back on Biden. And she knew that pressure would become unbearable.

Later that same day, July 10, Pelosi met with the president face-to-face. It was widely reported that she'd conducted her tête-à-tête with Biden over the phone. In fact, they met at the White House—not in the Oval Office, where they'd be seen, but in the residence. The meeting was prearranged before she went on *Morning Joe*. Pelosi had gone to extraordinary lengths to keep it secret. Months after the meeting, she still wouldn't publicly acknowledge it. Over lunch with me in his West Wing office, Jeff Zients only reluctantly confirmed that it had taken place. No one wanted to get out ahead of Nancy Pelosi.

Pelosi described her conversation with Biden to a friend: "We had a long talk about America." It was the kind of heartfelt, nostalgic conversation they'd had many times before, but this one was more poignant and emotional. The former speaker steered the president to the point. Based on polling done by the Democratic Party, he would lose by a much bigger margin than his advisers had been telling him—more than five points, she said, cocking an eyebrow.

Pelosi made her closing argument. If he decided to step aside, she told him, historians would call it one of the most courageous decisions ever made by a president.

Biden still had not budged. But Pelosi was certain she'd gotten through to him. She told her friend, "I was the only one who could send that message. He trusts me." She said this in a matter-of-fact, not boastful, way. Her bond with Biden was based on "what we've done together and our shared Catholic faith and our close family relationship. He trusts me in a way that he doesn't others."

That same day, *The New York Times* published an opinion piece that would prove to be explosive. A month earlier, the actor George Clooney had attended a glittery Hollywood fund-raiser for Biden's campaign in Los Angeles. Present were not only Clooney and Biden but actress Julia Roberts, late-night TV host Jimmy Kimmel, and Barack Obama. Clooney was shocked by how much the president had aged. And he wasn't the only one. Jon Favreau and Tommy Vietor, two of the "Pod Save Bros," also came away alarmed by Biden's condition.

Clooney's piece began: "I love Joe Biden." And then he dropped the hammer:

> But the one battle he cannot win is the fight against time. None of us can. It's devastating to say it, but the Joe Biden I was with three weeks ago at the fund-raiser was not the Joe "big F—-ing deal" Biden of 2010. He wasn't even the Joe Biden of 2020. He was the same man we all witnessed at the debate . . . most of our members of Congress are opting to wait and see if the dam breaks. But the dam has broken. We can put our heads in the sand and pray for a miracle in November, or we can speak the truth . . . Joe Biden is a hero; he saved democracy in 2020. We need him to do it again in 2024.

Clooney's shot across Biden's bow was a thunderbolt. When I asked him about it, Ted Kaufman was disgusted. "I don't care,

George, with all due respect," he snapped, mimicking what he would say to Clooney. "I know you're famous and you're important and people kiss your ass every day. But George, I'm just not interested!"

Not only had Clooney, the nation's most famous Democratic fundraiser, turned on the president but he'd reportedly consulted with someone before publishing the piece: Barack Obama. Had Clooney sought and received a green light from the former president? I asked Obama's former White House chief of staff, Bill Daley. "He wouldn't put a red light up," he said. "I'm sure that event in LA rattled them all."

The next morning, July 11, the co-anchor of MSNBC's *Morning Joe*, Mika Brzezinski, presided over one of the strangest segments in recent television history. After a taped report about Clooney's op-ed piece and his possible collusion with Obama, Brzezinski made it clear just who she thought had put Clooney up to writing the piece: "This wasn't George Clooney. Come on," she said, smiling. "It was not Matt Damon. It wasn't Julia Roberts either."

"Who do you think it was?" said her co-anchor and husband, Joe Scarborough, egging her on. "You can say the name. It's not Voldemort. Are you saying you think Barack Obama put him up to this?"

"I think that Barack Obama has a lot of influence and I think that there's a lot there."

The screen showed a photo of Obama and Biden.

"I tell you, there are two people in this picture," said Brzezinski. "And one has had a presidency that was absolutely, undeniably, historic."

"Well, I think you have two people that had extraordinary presidencies. . . ." said Scarborough.

"Oh, I'm sorry," Mika replied, "I mean in terms of *historic accomplishments.*"

It was a remarkable piece of television: Not only was a prominent television news anchor accusing Clooney of conspiring with Obama to drive Biden from the race, she was also saying that Obama's presidency had been a failure compared to his vice president's.

Mika and Joe were anchoring the show from Maine. As Brzezinski's extraordinary takedown of Clooney and Obama went on, correspondents Willie Geist and Mike Barnicle, on the set in New York City's Rockefeller Center, listened awkwardly. "What the fuck?" they thought. Before either one could say a word, a producer's voice came over their earpieces "Don't interrupt her. Don't interrupt her."

At 10:05 a.m., after *Morning Joe* had wrapped, one of the show's producers walked into his Manhattan apartment. His phone started buzzing and he answered. The voice was familiar.

"How the fuck could you let her link me with Barack Obama saying he made me write the op-ed?" It was George Clooney.

The producer pushed back. "Listen, I didn't do that," he said.

"You fucked me," Clooney shouted. "You're my friend. You should have stood up for me."

"George," the producer said, "this is not a fucking movie. There's no script. It's just not a movie where you go script page to script page."

"Fuck you!" Clooney replied.

"Fuck yourself!" said the producer.

The exchange of F-bombs lasted about five minutes before Clooney hung up. A few minutes later he called back for another round of cursing and arguing. The actor called a third time just after noon and the shouting match went on.

The producer had had enough. "This is a morning talk show on a cable channel," he shouted at Clooney. "Nobody gives a fuck if we say he should get out or if he should stay in. Nobody fucking cares. It's skywriting. It's fucking gone. George, I told you before, we'll try and take care of it tomorrow morning. I promise you."

"I don't know whether I trust you," Clooney replied.

"Well, fuck you," said the producer. "If you don't trust me, stop fucking calling me."

As THE STORM OVER BIDEN'S EMBATTLED CANDIDACY RAGED, Donald Trump was practically invisible. He'd been unusually silent, content to let Biden's troubles play out.

On July 11 at 7:40 a.m., Paul Manafort sent me a long, unprompted text message:

What happens if Biden is not the Nominee.

In the midst of all this drama, people are commenting on how serene Donald Trump has been. Well, he has many reasons.

He understands that the turmoil around Biden is nothing compared to what it will be like if "the mob" drives Biden out of the campaign.

To hear Manafort tell it, Trump couldn't wait to run against Harris. If Biden were driven from the ticket, Trump would paint Harris as the product of an illegal Democratic Party coup. Manafort continued:

At the core is the fact that the 14 million Democrats who voted in the Democratic primaries are told their vote is meaningless. This fact becomes the foundation of the Trump attack . . . once again, the Democrats have cheated.

. . . The real threat to Democracy is the crass disdain [of] the Democratic Establishment, Hollywood cabal, Wall St. donor class and the MSM (Main Stream Media, the elites) when they have their power base threatened

But did Trump and his aides really think voters would care about how Harris became the nominee? Maybe not, because in his next text message, Manafort was savoring the possibility that "after all of this public admission that the Democratic Establishment . . . knew Biden had serious mental illness but kept quiet until the dam burst at the Presidential debate, Biden remains the nominee. That one is too delicious."

ON JULY 13, 2024, A BRIGHT, CLOUDLESS SATURDAY AFTERNOON in rural Butler, Pennsylvania, Donald Trump, dressed in a blazer and red MAGA cap, addressed a throng of supporters from a stage draped with campaign bunting. The former president turned his head slightly to the right.

"If you want to really see something that's sad . . ." he said.

Suddenly Trump raised his hand to his ear.

A snapping, crackling sound filled the air.

He suddenly fell in a heap behind the podium—onlookers screamed.

On a rooftop a little more than a hundred meters away, a would-be assassin had opened fire.

"BLOOD ON EVERYONE IS JUST A MASSACRE."

Donald Trump lay on the floor of the rally stage in Butler, Pennsylvania, with four Secret Service agents on top of him. It was 6:13 p.m. on July 13, 2024, and the former president's face was smeared with blood, trickling from a wound on his right ear. One spectator lay dead and two others were severely injured. After the initial fusillade, which sounded like firecrackers, another shot rang out; a Secret Service sniper had shot Trump's assailant on a nearby rooftop, killing him instantly. Now Trump's security detail was waiting for a signal that it was safe to rush Trump to his armored SUV.

"Let's move!" shouted an agent.

Draped by his security guards, Trump rose to his feet. Then he raised his fist defiantly toward the cameras, not once but three times, each time mouthing the word "Fight!"

Trump's near-assassination was an appalling security failure. In broad daylight, a would-be assassin, armed with a semiautomatic rifle, had been able to climb onto a roof within range of the former president. Minutes before the shots were fired, a witness had tried to alert the Secret Service but to no avail. An investigation by the Senate's Permanent Subcommittee on Investigations, released on September 25, found that the incident was totally preventable, caused by a cascade of errors, a failure to communicate, and a total breakdown in the chain of command. Democratic senator Richard Blumenthal of Connecticut, the committee's chair, called the incident "a perfect storm of stunning failure."

But if his close brush with death gave the U.S. Secret Service a black eye, it was a political boon for Trump. Under fire, with his visceral instinct for political theater, he'd seized the moment, raising his fist and exhorting his followers, "Fight! Fight! Fight!" It would become Trump's new rallying cry, as much a part of his angry, defiant political brand as the fierce mugshot he'd posed for at Atlanta's Fulton County Jail, where he'd been arrested on August 24 for trying to overturn Georgia's election results.

For Trump, the botched assassination packed a one-two political punch. To evangelical Christians and many of his MAGA faithful, Trump's ordeal was nothing less than a religious revelation—a sign that he was the Chosen One. The godless political heathen had tried everything to stop him—slandering him, prosecuting him, suing him, cheating him, and by God, now they'd tried to kill him. Donald Trump, Jr., accused Democrats of inciting the attempt on his father's life with their inflammatory rhetoric. But Trump was invincible. It was hard to imagine a myth better suited to whip up the MAGA faithful. And the former president's political advisers saw something else: an opportunity to appeal beyond his base, a chance to introduce a new Trump.

There was historical precedent for this. Back in 1972, George Corley Wallace, the Democratic governor of Alabama and racist firebrand, had rocked the political world by riding a populist political movement to presidential primary victories across the country. His ardent supporters were the MAGA voters of their day: disillusioned, alienated working-class folks who were fed up with Washington's pointy-headed elites.

While campaigning in Laurel, Maryland, on May 15, 1972, Wallace was shot and severely wounded by a deranged gunman. Paralyzed from the waist down, Wallace had no chance of capturing the Democratic nomination, but his near-death experience led to a remarkable transformation. Once a champion of segregation "now, tomorrow, and forever," Wallace renounced his racist views and pledged to repair the damage he'd spent his career inflicting on Black Americans.

No one expected Donald Trump to undergo a similar road-to-Damascus conversion. But after *his* near-death experience, stories began to spread that Trump was a changed man. The next day after his wounding, Bret Baier of Fox News reported that the presumptive GOP nominee had called in by phone. "He . . . called for unity in the country," Baier reported.

Even Melania Trump signaled a new, gentler tone, releasing a pleading letter: "Let us reunite. Now," she wrote, proclaiming that "differing opinions, policy, and political games are inferior to love."

The former president practically declared that he'd been resurrected. "I'm not supposed to be here, I'm supposed to be dead," he told the *New York Post* on July 14 on his campaign plane. Less than twenty-four hours after he'd literally dodged a bullet, Trump was headed to Milwaukee, Wisconsin, for the four-day Republican National Convention. He was having his nomination speech rewritten to reflect his new outlook. "I had all prepared an extremely tough speech," Trump said. "But I threw it away." He promised "to try to unite our country." The unveiling of the new Trump would come on July 18, the convention's final day, when he would accept the GOP nomination.

The Milwaukee convention represented Trump's political and spiritual coronation. Many of his followers believed his survival was divinely ordained. As Anthony Lane wrote in *The New Yorker*, "It was as if some ancient prophecy had been fulfilled—as if the stalwarts of the Republican Party had expected not only that a heinous act would be committed against their champion but also that he would, being Trump, survive and rise. The Convention was always going to be a crowning. Now, however, thanks to his deliverance, it had swelled into something more. It was *Easter*."

It was also a brash, over-the-top advertisement for Trump. Arriving at Milwaukee's FiServ Forum on Monday evening, the prospective nominee, wearing a rectangular white bandage on his right ear, strode dramatically down a long corridor, as Lee Greenwood sang the old Reagan campaign song "God Bless the U.S.A." Climbing stairs to the next level, Trump paused and punched his fist in the air three times, his back-from-the-dead salute.

Then Trump took a seat from which, mostly in silence, he would behold the proceedings from on high over the next three days. He wore a self-satisfied expression, like a tribal king observing human sacrifices.

Staring at him, with an adoring look, like Nancy Reagan gazing at Ronnie, was Trump's vice-presidential nominee, J.D. Vance.

Trump's choice of Vance as his VP was surprising. For one thing, his pedigree was decidedly un-MAGA-like: A graduate of Yale Law School, Vance had been a protégé of the Silicon Valley billionaire entrepreneur Peter Thiel. Moreover, Vance had savaged Trump in the past. He'd called him "America's Hitler"—and himself a "Never Trump guy." He said Trump was peddling "cultural heroin." But since writing *Hillbilly Elegy*, his bestselling book about the forgotten rural middle class, Vance had evidently had a change of heart, a come-to-the-Orange-Jesus moment. After winning a Senate seat from Ohio with Trump's backing, Vance made a Faustian bargain and dedicated himself whole hog to the MAGA agenda. Now he'd been richly rewarded with the second spot on the GOP ticket.

For his part, Trump rarely blamed people who'd attacked him in the past—as long as they bent the knee to him going forward. Vance had pledged allegiance to Trump over the Constitution; he said, for example, that unlike Mike Pence, he would have found a way to reject Joe Biden's slate of electors and prevent the legitimate transfer of power on January 6, 2021. To a transactional creature like Trump, that was money in the cash register. And Vance was not only loyal to a fault, he was also good-looking and smooth on television, important qualifications in Trump's world.

The launch of the Trump-Vance ticket in Milwaukee went more or less according to plan. Manafort made an appearance on the second day, surveying the colorful scene from an upper balcony. The mood on the floor was somehow both angry and festive. Speakers included former candidates Vivek Ramaswamy and Tim Scott and the entertainment featured Chris Janson and Kid Rock. The convention was more about testosterone than policy. At one point, Trump was introduced to James Brown's "It's a Man's Man's Man's World." The Trump mania-fest would culminate on Day Four, nomination night, with the dramatic appearance of Terry Gene Bollea, aka Hulk Hogan, the retired professional wrestler. The Hulk riled up the audience by ripping his shirt to shreds and yelling about Trumpamaniacs.

Everyone there seemed dead certain that Trump would be the next president of the United States. Speaker after speaker argued that his victory had been inevitable the moment he picked himself up off that rally stage and raised his fist in the air. The election would be just a formality.

On Day Four of the event, Trump strode to the podium to deliver his acceptance speech. Rewritten to convey a kinder, gentler candidate, his address had been loaded into the teleprompter. "Friends, delegates and fellow citizens, I stand before you here this evening with a message of confidence, strength, and hope," Trump began. "The discord and division in our society must be healed. We must heal it quickly . . . I am running to be president for all of America, not half of America because there is no victory in winning for half of America."

So far he sounded nothing like the embittered and divisive Trump of the campaign trail. The newly anointed GOP nominee vividly described his close brush with death less than a week before. "Bullets were continuing to fly as very brave Secret Service agents rushed to the stage, and they really did—they rushed to the stage," Trump said. "There was blood pouring everywhere and yet in a certain way I felt very safe because I had God on my side." The crowd roared. "I stand before you in this arena only by the grace of almighty God . . . I raised my right arm and looked at the thousands of thousands of people that were breathlessly waiting and started shouting 'Fight, Fight, Fight!'" The crowd broke into applause, echoing the chant.

Trump paid tribute to Corey Comperatore, the spectator who'd been killed in the July 13 attack.

And then, as if bored by his good behavior, the former president veered off the track. Ignoring the teleprompter, he launched a partisan attack on his enemies. "The Democrat party should immediately stop weaponizing," he complained. "In fact, *I* am the one saving democracy for the people of our country." He railed about the "fake documents case," "partisan witch hunts," and "crazy Nancy Pelosi." And then he segued to one of his favorite schticks (and a crowd favorite, too): a meandering riff about "the late, great Hannibal Lecter."

So much for the plan, drawn up by Susie Wiles and Chris LaCivita, to appeal to undecided voters with a unifying message. Trump's nomination speech was a rare chance to persuade millions of television viewers that he was no longer a vindictive agent of retribution. But Trump was who he was.

There would be no new Trump after all.

JOE BIDEN HAD JUST FINISHED A RADIO INTERVIEW AT A MEXIcan restaurant in Las Vegas, Nevada. It was July 17, 2024, and he was scheduled to appear that afternoon at a campaign rally sponsored by UnidosUS, a Latino civil rights group. It was one more chance for the president to demonstrate that he was strong enough, physically and cognitively, to continue his reelection campaign. Biden had felt lousy all morning—and suddenly he felt much worse. He slipped into the restaurant's kitchen, where he was given a COVID test. It came back positive.

There was nothing to do but cancel the rally and head home. Biden and his aides decided to fly to Dover Air Force Base; from there he would head to his house in Rehoboth Beach and recuperate in isolation over the weekend.

Biden's COVID diagnosis was a body blow to his faltering campaign. On the flight to Dover, the president put up a brave front. Fully masked, he left his cabin and wandered the aisle, peppering the staff with questions. "What's the plan for the next few days?" he asked. "I'm going to be down, but are you guys working on this?"

But the president's aides had a sinking feeling on the long flight. One of them thought about how unfair life had been to Biden. He'd been fighting tooth and nail, clawing his way back to life as a candidate—and now this. "I think folks on the plane kind of knew where this was going to end up," an aide told me months later. "After getting out there and doing all these rallies and working his ass off for a few weeks, he gets COVID. You know, every time we've climbed up the hill, something else happens."

At 11:20 p.m., Air Force One rolled to a stop on the tarmac at Dover Air Force Base. Soon Biden appeared at the top of the stairs. He started down the steps unsteadily, grasping the rail with his right hand. After just two steps he stopped. Biden raised his left hand as if to wave and turned his head slowly from side to side. He took two more steps and stopped again. The president stared straight ahead. He looked lost. Finally, he descended to the tarmac.

"I saw him get off the plane," said Peter Baker, the *New York Times* chief Washington correspondent. "He seemed confused. He didn't seem to know where he was. He didn't seem to know what was going on. He looked as frail and wasted as I've ever seen him."

A Secret Service agent helped Biden into his armored SUV. The motorcade pulled away slowly.

Starkly contrasting images of the two presidential candidates made for a devastating split-screen: Trump pumping his fist; Biden grasping a handrail.

• • •

"BLOOD ON EVERYONE IS JUST A MASSACRE."

THE NEXT DAY, THURSDAY, JULY 18, I TEXTED PAUL MANAFORT.

Are you guys prepping for Harris? Or do you think Joe stays?

Manafort: "We are prepped for Harris."

Despite all the pressure on Biden to abdicate, there was still no hint that he was giving up the fight. I texted Manafort back:

"Joe's still in, I think."

Manafort: "Out on Monday."

I wondered how he could be sure. "I'll take that bet," I texted.

Almost anyone would have taken that bet. Did the Trump campaign know something I didn't? That was unlikely. Even Biden's inner circle didn't foresee the stunning turn of events that would unfold over the next few days. One of the president's closest confidants told me, "If you'd said going into the weekend, is he going to be running on Monday morning?, I would have said yes."

The weekend of July 20–21, 2024, would prove to be seminal, a hinge of American history.

As the president convalesced at his house in Rehoboth Beach, the cries for Biden to give up reelection grew louder. On July 17, Adam Schiff issued a statement calling on Biden to step aside; it was lost on no one, least of all the president, that the congressman from Burbank, California, favored to replace Dianne Feinstein in the upcoming U.S. senatorial election, wouldn't have done this without his mentor Nancy Pelosi's blessing.

Schiff was the twenty-third member of Congress, and the

most prominent, to call publicly for Biden to withdraw. That same day, at the behest of party leaders Jeffries and Schumer, the Democratic National Committee scrapped a plan to nominate Biden in advance of the Democratic convention.

On Friday, July 19, Ron Klain called the president. They talked about the growing pressure on Biden to withdraw. Klain urged him to resist it. "That's my intention," Biden told him.

For the next forty-eight hours, Joe Biden went radio silent. Other than his Secret Service detail, the only people at the Rehoboth house were Jill Biden, Annie Tomasini, and Anthony Bernal. No one knew if Biden was considering abdicating—but back at the White House, one aide thought the president's silence was telling. "He's somebody who checks in pretty frequently and wants to know what's going on and wants to talk things through," he said. "When things went quiet, I think we knew he was seriously thinking about it."

On Saturday morning, July 20, Mike Donilon and Steve Ricchetti arrived at the president's beach house. With more than sixty years of service to Joe Biden between them, Donilon and Ricchetti had been at his side through innumerable political and personal crises—from hard-fought victories to agonizing defeats. They'd seen everything.

But the president's men had never faced a crisis as profound as this. Ricchetti, bearing polling data, went first. He told the president that while he was down by a few points nationally, and more in the battleground states, he was within the historical margin to come back and win. Public opinion wasn't the obstacle; the party was. Most of its leaders were against him. "There's a path for you to win the nomination and the presidency," Ricchetti told the president, "but it will be brutal, and you will have to wage a fierce, lonely fight against your own party. This could hurt your reputation for being a unifying commander-in-chief that is core to you."

In fact, the path to a Biden victory was so narrow as to be almost nonexistent; Trump's lead in the battleground states was insurmountable. But even at this late hour Ricchetti and Donilon were softpedaling this hard reality. What the president's aides could not sugarcoat was the fact that the party's leaders were about to publicly renounce Biden. "They knew the honeymoon was over that weekend," a source close to the leadership told me. "Pelosi, Schumer, and Jeffries would have all been publicly calling for him to get out. And you knew it was going to happen when Adam Schiff went out. He does not sh-- without Nancy Pelosi approving it. So the moment he said that, you knew the game was over."

As the walls closed in on Biden, he felt abandoned. It wasn't just Nancy Pelosi and the Obamas and the party leaders that he'd lost faith in; he wasn't even sure his White House staff had his back. "He was like 'What happened here?'" said a Biden confidant. "'Why was there no one on my side?' And he got very focused on whether or not people were being loyal to him inside the building. I think he lost confidence in the people right around him."

Biden knew that Donilon, Ricchetti, and Klain were committed to his reelection; they would have died on that hill. But the president wasn't so sure about everyone else.

Biden turned to Donilon, his longtime wordsmith. "If I were to drop out," he said, "what would it look like and sound like?" Donilon said he'd knock out a draft of a withdrawal statement. Biden told him, "I want to sleep on it."

At about noon the next day, Sunday, Zients was in his West Wing office when his phone lit up. "I was sitting here doing my normal Sunday routine because I come in every Sunday and organize the upcoming week," he told me three months later, over lunch in his office. It was the president. "I've decided not to run," Biden told his chief of staff. Zients tried to engage him. "That lasted about a minute because he said, 'What I really want to talk about is how do we have as productive a six-month period—that's how much time was left—as we've had in the first three and a half years.' He said, 'I want a new 180-day plan that reflects the fact that we're no longer running.'" Biden ticked through his priorities for the remainder of his presidency: passing legislation that would lower costs, protecting personal freedoms and civil rights, and addressing national security issues: Gaza, Ukraine, and China.

There remained the question: Who, if anyone, should Biden endorse as his successor? It was a momentous question. Indeed, everything was riding on Biden's successor—not only the outcome of the 2024 presidential election but the fate of Biden's agenda, his historical legacy, and the future of the party.

Kamala Harris was the logical choice. Biden's endorsement would almost certainly make her the nominee. But Harris was a risky choice. Her 2020 presidential campaign had been a fiasco. Biden needed to know she had a chance of beating Trump.

Ten days earlier, on July 11, *The New York Times* had reported that the Biden campaign's analytics unit had conducted polling on how Harris would perform at the top of the ticket. No one in the Harris camp had been told about it. What was the purpose of that polling—if not to provide the results to Biden? On the weekend of July 20–21, Ricchetti and Donilon almost surely discussed those results with the president—though the White House wouldn't confirm it. "Something that sensitive wouldn't have been done on a lark by the analytics department," said a senior Harris adviser. "Biden wanted some assurance that she would be competitive."

Some prominent Democrats, who dreaded a Harris-led ticket, wanted an open primary of some kind, shortened because of the calendar. One option that had been floated was a series of televised town halls, in which the party's up-and-coming stars could contend for the nomination. No one knew exactly how that would work—but James Carville had suggested that former presidents could act as moderators.

Biden thought an open primary at this stage of the race was a half-baked, half-assed idea that might alienate Black voters and fail to produce a better candidate. And he was right; financially, legally, and politically, an open primary was unworkable, a nonstarter. "It continues to boggle my mind," a senior member of the Democratic National Committee (DNC) told me, "how very senior politicians don't understand how the DNC and related matters work." And yet Nancy Pelosi was said to want a primary. Barack Obama wanted one, too. And he was thought to favor a governor, not Harris, as the nominee.

But the decision was Biden's alone to make. And the only counsel he was taking was from Ricchetti and Donilon.

Just after he spoke to Zients, Biden called Kamala Harris.

The vice president, wearing sweatpants and a Howard University hoodie, was in the kitchen of the mansion at the U.S. Naval Observatory in Northwest Washington, D.C. The second gentleman, Doug Emhoff, was in California. Harris's niece Meena was visiting and her two daughters, Harris's grand nieces, were sitting down to do a jigsaw puzzle. Her cell phone buzzed and she answered it. "Hello, Mr. President," she said.

"Listen," said Biden. "I've decided I'm not going to run." Harris sounded dumbfounded. She replied, "Are you sure? Are you sure you want to do that?" The president was sure. Biden hung up—but he called back a few minutes later. The president told Harris that the White House would release a letter announcing his decision soon—and he would endorse her by tweet fifteen minutes later.

From the moment Biden imploded during the CNN debate, Harris had been his staunch defender. In public she'd faced down his detractors, calling his performance just a bad night. In private she helped him strategize on how to remain in the race. Most important, there was not even a whisper that Harris had spoken to anyone about taking Biden's place on the ticket. But in fact, she'd been reaching out secretly to prepare for this moment.

The vice president was navigating a political minefield; the slightest misstep, any hint that she was plotting to replace the president, could have been politically fatal. But while Harris was lying low, her political operation was working behind the scenes. Her chief of staff, Lorraine Voles, had been thinking about a contingency like this since November 19, 2021. That was when President Biden, under Section 3 of the Twenty-Fifth Amendment, had voluntarily transferred his powers and duties to Harris while he underwent a colonoscopy. It concentrated Voles's mind. She and her staff needed to be ready for anything.

Still, replacing Biden on the ticket was a lot more complicated than being acting president for a day. To prepare for it, Harris's team launched a stealth operation; they recruited people with no direct connection to Harris or her campaign.

On Thursday, July 18, a veteran Democratic campaign operative got a call from Stephanie Schriock, the former head of EMILYs LIST. "I got a call to help the Harris campaign come up with a 'if he drops out plan,'" this operative told me. "'Can you take a look at all the rules and help us determine what we would actually need to do in terms of signatures?' They 100% did not know at that point. They were like, 'We just feel like we should put a plan in place. Maybe something happens.'"

It was critical that these efforts not be traced back to Harris or her staff. "We were all very careful that this was not Kamala," said the operative. "This was, 'if someone [Biden] wants to drop out, we desperately want a woman president and us women have to be there.' That was the framing."

Schriock and other Harris allies were also wrangling prominent Democratic senators to make a promise: If Biden didn't drop out by Monday, they would call on him publicly to step aside.

Now that Biden's abdication had actually come to pass, Harris would have to seize the nomination. And that meant winning over state party leaders and labor unions and reproductive rights groups and super delegates and state delegations. Harris had struggled with staff turnover during her first two years in office—but by 2024 she'd assembled a strong team, led by Voles; Sheila Nix, a senior adviser; Kirsten Allen, her communications director; and Brian Fallon, her senior communications adviser. They now activated a formidable political machine. "There was a political operation in place that was minding her Ps and Qs well ahead of the ticket switch," said an adviser. "We just were able to immediately utilize it for the sake of a whipping operation to secure the nomination."

At around 1 p.m., Jeff Zients called Ron Klain. "Hey, the president's getting out shortly," Zients told him. "He's not running for reelection."

For Klain, this was a gut punch. "Jeff, that's too bad," he replied. "I think that's a mistake. I think this was an avoidable tragedy."

Zients said, "Well, he's decided. We're going to put out a statement shortly."

Klain replied: "Okay."

Klain was one of Biden's true believers. In a conversation six weeks later, I asked him if he really thought the president could have prevailed in a battle for the nomination; even with the support of the Progressive Caucus, he'd be up against Nancy Pelosi, Chuck Schumer, Hakeem Jeffries, and Barack Obama. "That's a pretty bloody fight, isn't it?" I asked him.

"It's a very bloody fight," Klain said. But surrender was bloody, too. "Maybe the president didn't want to make the fight. But blood on everyone is not a fight at all. It's just a massacre."

At 1:45 p.m., the president conducted a conference call with his senior advisers from both the White House and campaign. Ricchetti, Donilon, Zients, and Klain already knew about his decision, but another member of Biden's team was about to get the news one minute before the rest of the world: Anita Dunn. For one of Biden's most powerful advisers, this was a remarkable fall from grace.

Biden had soured on Dunn. She and her husband, Bob Bauer, had gotten crosswise with his son Hunter; they'd argued that his public travails were hurting his father politically and that he should lower his profile. Hunter was furious and so was his father. Now, as the party deserted him, Biden couldn't shake his hunch that Dunn was more loyal to Obama. "He felt very betrayed by Obama and she represented that in his head," said a Biden confidant. "The president lost faith in Anita."

At 1:46 p.m., the White House released Biden's announcement that he was stepping away from the ticket. Twenty-seven minutes later, at 2:13 p.m., Biden sent out a tweet endorsing Harris.

Joe Biden looks on as President Donald Trump greets his predecessor Barack Obama during his 2017 inauguration. Biden never forgave Obama for anointing Hillary Clinton as the Democratic nominee. *Credit: David Hume Kennerly/Center for Creative Photography/University of Arizona*

Flanked by President Obama and his wife, Dr. Jill Biden, in the White House Rose Garden, Vice President Joe Biden announces that he won't run for president in 2016. Asked later about his decision, he said: "I regret it every day." © *Win McNamee/Getty Images*

President Trump and his wife, Melania, at Joint Base Andrews after refusing to attend Joe Biden's inauguration on January 20, 2021. "Goodbye, we love you," he told a small band of supporters. "We will be back in some form."
Credit: A1C Essence Myricks / U.S. Air Force Photo

Jared Kushner and Ivanka Trump in North Charleston, South Carolina. Trump's most powerful advisers asked for my advice on how to navigate a chaotic, faction-ridden White House.
Credit: Ryan Johnson

Brad Parscale, Trump's six-foot-eight-inch-tall 2016 digital director and 2020 campaign manager, was sacked after going on a lavish spending spree. "Height is not depth," quipped an adviser.
Credit: Diarmuid Greene / Web Summit via Sportsfile

Jennifer O'Malley Dillon, who ran Biden's winning 2020 campaign and would be tapped to run his 2024 race, was an organizational genius and badass taskmaster who could make grown men and women cry. © *The Washington Post/ Getty Images*

Biden on the campaign trail in 2020. Four years later, during his reelection race, aides privately confessed: "We had this great excuse of the basement, of COVID, to keep him out of the public eye. We no longer have that excuse. What do we do?" *Credit: David Hume Kennerly/Center for Creative Photography/University of Arizona*

Rioters besiege the U.S. Capitol on January 6, 2021. Biden, convinced that Trump and his MAGA movement would quickly fade, was shocked by their lasting power. *Credit: TapTheForwardAssist / Wikipedia / CC BY-SA 4.0*

Chris LaCivita and Susie Wiles, cochairs of Trump's 2024 campaign. LaCivita, a master of the dark art of negative campaigning, would help sink Kamala Harris with an ad attacking taxpayer-financed transgender surgery on prison inmates. © *AP Photo/Alex Brandon*

Wiles and Trump at an NFL game. The daughter of Pat Summerall, a famous television sportscaster who was also an alcoholic, Wiles knew how to handle difficult men. "She is an expert in unstable, dysfunctional, famous men," said a GOP operative. © *AP Photo/Evan Vucci, Pool*

Senior advisers Mike Donilon and Steve Ricchetti trail Joe Biden on the White House grounds. Loyal, insular, and bound by decades of service to the president, they couldn't accept the fact that he was too old to run for reelection. © *AP Photo/Andrew Harnik*

Kamala Harris and Joe Biden at a 9/11 memorial in New York City in 2024. The vice president was careful not to be caught plotting to replace him at the top of the ticket. But when Biden suddenly stepped aside, her political machine was ready.
Credit: Official White House Photo by Adam Schultz

Donald Trump and Joe Biden at the history-changing CNN debate, June 27, 2024. After Biden imploded, despite days of debate prep, his distraught sister, Valerie, called a friend and screamed: "What did they do to my brother at Camp David?" *Credit: David Hume Kennerly/Center for Creative Photography/University of Arizona*

Chris LaCivita in the post-debate spin room. The last thing the Trump campaign wanted was for Joe Biden to drop out of the 2024 race. © *Bloomberg/Getty Images*

George Clooney meets with President Barack Obama at the White House in October, 2010. After the actor published an op-ed piece on July 10, 2024, urging Joe Biden to abdicate, anchor Mika Brzezinski suggested on MSNBC's Morning Joe that Clooney had colluded with Obama. This prompted an F-bomb-laden shouting match between the actor and a Morning Joe producer. *Credit: Photograph by Pete Souza, White House Photographer*

ABC News anchor George Stephanopoulos and Joe Biden on the set. After his disastrous debate with Trump, Biden tried to salvage his candidacy by doing interviews—to no avail. *Credit: ABC News via Getty Images*

Nearly killed by a would-be assassin, Trump rises to his feet and raises his fist, mouthing, "Fight, fight, fight." It would become his campaign's defiant rallying cry. © *Rebecca Droke/Getty Images*

Arriving at Dover Air Force Base on July 17 after an aborted campaign trip to California, Joe Biden looks lost and befuddled on the steps of Air Force One. © *AP Photo/Susan Walsh*

Trump and his vice-presidential nominee, J.D. Vance, applaud a speaker at the Republican National Convention (RNC) in Milwaukee, Wisconsin. The testosterone-fueled event was Trump's political and spiritual coronation. *Credit: David Hume Kennerly/Center for Creative Photography/University of Arizona*

Joe Biden's beach house in Rehoboth, Delaware. Stricken with COVID and feeling betrayed by party leaders and allies, the president would retreat here to make a history-altering decision.
Credit: RoseForEmilyGrierson / Wikipedia / Creative Commons

Paul Manafort surveys the arena at the RNC. Trump's 2016 campaign chairman, sentenced to seven years in prison for bank fraud and other crimes but pardoned by the boss, played an under-the-radar role in his 2024 presidential campaign. *Credit: David Hume Kennerly/ Center for Creative Photography/ University of Arizona*

After his attempted assassination, Trump promised a kinder, gentler persona. But during his nomination speech, he veers off the teleprompter to attack his enemies and riff about Hannibal Lecter. There would be no new Trump after all. *Credit: David Hume Kennerly/ Center for Creative Photography/ University of Arizona*

Trump's family and friends at the RNC. Front row (l to r): Usha Vance, J.D. Vance, Melania Trump, and Eric Trump. Back row: Kimberly Guilfoyle, Lara Trump, Jared Kushner, and Ivanka Trump. Ivanka and Jared sat out the 2024 campaign. *Credit: David Hume Kennerly/ Center for Creative Photography/ University of Arizona*

Bandaged after being wounded by a would-be assassin's bullet, Trump celebrates with Melania and Ivanka at the RNC. *Credit: David Hume Kennerly/Center for Creative Photography/University of Arizona*

Donald Trump pumps a fist upon arriving at the convention. *Credit: David Hume Kennerly/Center for Creative Photography/University of Arizona*

Hulk Hogan, the retired professional wrestler, riles up the MAGA faithful at the RNC. *Credit: David Hume Kennerly/ Center for Creative Photography/University of Arizona*

On the opening night of the Democratic National Convention (DNC) in Chicago, Illinois (l to r): Second Gentleman Douglas Emhoff, Vice President Kamala Harris, Minnesota governor Tim Walz, and Gwen Walz applaud Joe Biden.

Joe Biden speaks to the DNC, ending his fifty-two-year political career. Quoting the song "American Anthem," he concludes: "Let me know in my heart when my days are through, America. America, I gave my best to you." *Credit: David Hume Kennerly/Center for Creative Photography/University of Arizona*

Kamala Harris reacts to Biden's goodbye speech. *Credit: David Hume Kennerly/Center for Creative Photography/University of Arizona*

During Biden's farewell speech, I spot House Speaker Emerita Nancy Pelosi, who'd been instrumental in forcing him to step aside, watching from the arena floor. *Credit: David Hume Kennerly/Center for Creative Photography/University of Arizona*

On the DNC's first night, eight years after her ill-fated nomination, Hillary Clinton acknowledges her fans after delivering a speech that rocked the arena. *Credit: David Hume Kennerly/Center for Creative Photography/University of Arizona*

Accepting the Democratic nomination, Kamala Harris gives a rousing speech aimed at rallying Democrats and wooing undecided Republicans. *Credit: David Hume Kennerly/Center for Creative Photography/ University of Arizona*

Visiting the New York delegation, I notice Governor Kathy Hochul (in red) and attorney general Letitia James sitting together. James won a $454-million civil suit against Donald Trump.

On election night at the Palm Beach County Convention Center, President-elect Trump salutes his followers. © *AP Photo/Evan Vucci*

Usha Vance, Vice President–elect J.D. Vance, Ivanka Trump, and Jared Kushner celebrate Trump's 2024 election victory, the greatest comeback in American political history. © *AP Photo/Lynne Sladky*

On election night at her alma mater, Howard University, in Washington, D.C., Kamala Harris's faithful react to spokesman Cedric Richmond's news that she won't be appearing to declare victory that night. *Credit: David Hume Kennerly/Center for Creative Photography/University of Arizona*

Remnants of an election celebration that wasn't to be.

After her concession speech the day after the 2024 election, Kamala Harris and Doug Emhoff head home. *Credit: David Hume Kennerly/Center for Creative Photography/University of Arizona*

After taking the oath of office in the Capitol Rotunda (indoors, due to frigid weather), Donald Trump delivers his inaugural address. His campaign manager and incoming White House chief of staff, Susie Wiles (in white), applauds. For all their accomplishments in office, history will remember Joe Biden and Kamala Harris for having set the stage for Trump's triumphant return. *Photograph © Shawn Thew/Pool photo via AP*

"BLOOD ON EVERYONE IS JUST A MASSACRE."

By now, a dozen Harris advisers had joined the vice president around her dining room table at the Naval Observatory. Laptops open, cell phones buzzing, they were wrangling support from around the country.

Suddenly Harris shouted: "Could someone please get hold of my husband?" She'd called the second gentleman three times and got his voicemail—he was riding a bike at Soul Cycle in San Francisco. Next Harris stepped into the turret of the castle-like mansion so she could speak without being overheard.

First she called Bill and Hillary Clinton. They offered their support and an immediate endorsement. Next she called Barack and Michelle Obama. The forty-fourth president was supportive—but said he wanted to wait a few days before endorsing her to avoid the appearance of an abrupt coronation. (By now, Obama evidently preferred the *appearance* of a process to an actual open primary.) Michelle Obama was not only all-in, she offered to campaign with Harris—something she'd refused to do for Joe Biden.

At campaign headquarters in Wilmington, Delaware, heads were spinning. With a new person at the top of the ticket, Jen O'Malley Dillon didn't know if she still had a job. "There was a little bit of chaos, people kind of trying to grab things and take power a little bit," said a senior campaign adviser. Suddenly O'Malley Dillon's cell phone went off. It was the vice president. "I need you," Harris told her. "I want you to stay on. This is going to be hard and not perfect. We have 107 days—and it's got to be good enough." This didn't sound like Harris. "For someone who's kind of a perfectionist," said one of her advisers, "that was a big step for her. She said she wasn't going to put up with any drama—we're not going to have any of that. We don't have time for it."

Harris's next calls were to potential political rivals for the nomination: governors Roy Cooper of North Carolina, Josh Shapiro of Pennsylvania, Gretchen Whitmer of Michigan, JB Pritzker of Illinois, and Gavin Newsom of California. Some of them asked Harris what the "process" would be. Harris replied crisply that it should be settled in the normal way: Whoever earned a majority of the pledged delegates would win the nomination. Period.

Cooper, Whitmer, Shapiro, and Newsom offered Harris their support that same day. Another potential rival, Arizona senator Mark Kelly, followed suit.

The enormity of what was happening struck Kamala Harris early in the afternoon. It was a moment none of Harris's advisers and friends would forget. The vice president called her pastor and put him on speakerphone. Eighty-three-year-old Reverend Amos C. Brown led Harris, Voles, Nix, and Allen in prayer—asking God for guidance and wisdom, for the good of the country. "What does the Lord require of you but to do justice," he said, reciting from the Bible verse, Micah 6:8, "and to love kindness, and to walk humbly with your God?" The vice president was verklempt, in tears. "She welled up for sure," said an adviser. "We all did."

LATER THAT AFTERNOON, RON KLAIN SPOKE TO BIDEN BY PHONE. "He definitely was feeling isolated," Klain said. "He kept saying, 'You know, I just don't know who's on my side, really.'"

It was his perceived betrayal by Barack Obama that stung Biden most of all. It wasn't just the damaging leaks about his infirmity that he knew had come from Obama's people. Nor did Biden really care whether Obama had given George Clooney a green light to write that brutal op-ed piece. What hurt was that Obama hadn't picked up the phone and called him. "The one thing that still gnaws at him," one of Biden's close friends told me, "is the fact that Obama never called him to have misgivings about his candidacy—to say, 'You know, Jeez, Joe, are you sure you're up to it?' None of that."

Obama *had* called Biden early on, right after the debate with Trump; he'd said don't worry, we've all had lousy debate nights. But afterward, as the pressure on Biden to step away grew to a crescendo, during the days before he retreated to Rehoboth, Biden had heard nothing from the former president. "The thing that still annoys the shit out of him," said Biden's friend, "is the fact that Barack Obama never called him."

That evening, still miserable with COVID, Joe Biden retreated to the bedroom of his beach house. The president was alone with his thoughts. "Depending on what day of the week it is," said his friend, "depending on whether he sees Trump on a video replay at night, he'll say, 'I could have beat that fucking guy.' But he couldn't have. I don't know if in his lifetime he'll ever really come to that conclusion. But that debate was it for him. You cannot erase that image in the minds of millions of voters."

By 10 p.m., at the Naval Observatory, jigsaw pieces were still strewn across the kitchen table. But the puzzle of Harris's nomination had been solved. She'd called more than a hundred people. Not a single potential rival had challenged her. JB Pritzker offered his endorsement the next day. By Monday morning, Harris had the backing of a majority of Democrats in Congress. Within forty-eight hours she had the support of most delegates to the upcoming Democratic convention. A senior adviser summed up Harris's two-day campaign to secure the nomination, a political tour de force. "A lot of people were like, 'There's not a process. We need a process.' Well, there *is* a process. The process is getting the delegates to commit. We just needed to do it and we did it."

Meanwhile, excitement among the Democratic rank and file was exploding. It was as though, with Biden's withdrawal, a party that had been holding its breath could suddenly exhale. Harris's approval rating had shot up sixteen points, an unprecedent leap for a presidential candidate. New voter registration spiked and volunteers poured into Harris for President (formerly Biden-Harris) offices across the country. In two days, 50,000 volunteers had signed up; a week later, the number would grow to 360,000. Money poured in—$81 million within twenty-four hours—inspired by Zoom calls for Harris organized by "#WinWithBlackWomen," "White Women for Kamala," and "White Dudes for Harris."

On July 24, I spoke by Zoom with Manafort again. He claimed that the Trump campaign was ready and eager to run against Harris. "A couple of weeks before, we pivoted on getting ready to do a Harris ad campaign," he said. "We had commercials in the can." But Trump and his team seemed utterly unprepared for her. At his first appearance after Harris's ascension, Trump was flat-footed, fumbling for a line of attack.

In truth, Trump couldn't get over the fact that he was no longer running against Biden. He railed at his aides about how unfair it was that he couldn't run against Sleepy Joe. It was worse than unfair, he said, it was crooked. The elites had stolen the nomination from Biden. "So now I have to win *three* times?" he complained to Manafort. According to Trump's fuzzy math, he'd won against Biden in the 2020 election, beaten him again in the June 2024 debate . . . and now he had to defeat *her*.

On Monday, the day after Biden's abdication, Harris paid a visit to campaign headquarters in Wilmington, Delaware. It was July 22, 2024, 106 days before election day. As Harris waited off stage, Julie Chávez Rodriguez introduced Joe Biden, who'd called in from his Rehoboth house. "The name has changed at the top of the ticket, but the mission hasn't changed," he told them in a disembodied voice. "If we don't win this thing, it's all in jeopardy." Then Harris made her entrance to chants of "Kamala!" Biden was still listening in. "I'm watching you, kid, I'm watching you, kid. I love you," he said.

"It is my great honor to have Joe's endorsement in this race," Harris told the campaign staff. "And it is my intention to go out and earn this nomination and to win."

The Harris campaign unfolded at warp speed. On July 23, the vice president secured enough delegates to clinch the nomination. That same day, at her first rally, in Milwaukee, Wisconsin, she took the stage to the booming soundtrack of Beyoncé's "Freedom," as the crowd chanted, "Kamala, Kamala!" Her reception was electric.

Harris reminded the audience of her history as a prosecutor and attorney general. "In those roles I took on perpetrators of all kinds," she said. "Predators who abused women. Fraudsters who ripped off consumers. Cheaters who broke the rules for their own gain. So hear me when I say: *I know Donald Trump's type.*" The crowd roared. The line was the result of a brainstorming session between the VP and her staff.

Harris was hitting her stride, speaking with a fluency and

authenticity she'd never shown during her 2019 presidential campaign. On Friday, July 25, in a videotaped phone call, Barack Obama finally gave Harris his endorsement, calling her a "Happy Warrior." Trump's pollster Tony Fabrizio sent out an unusual memo, warning of "the Harris Honeymoon." He wrote: "There is no question that Harris will get her bump earlier than the Democrat's [sic] convention. And that bump is likely to start showing itself over the next few days and will last until the race settles back down . . . the Democrats and the MSM [mainstream media] will try and tout these polls as proof that the race has changed. But the fundamentals of the race stay the same . . ."

For Harris, the fundamentals were daunting. Sixty-five percent of Americans believed the nation was on the wrong track. The Democratic National Convention loomed, beginning on August 19. Harris and her supporters were riding a wave of enthusiasm and hope toward Chicago. But others were also headed there. They were demanding that Harris do something to end the bloodshed in Gaza.

"THIS COUNTRY IS NOTHING LIKE IT WAS IN 1968."

At 4 a.m. on a night illuminated by a full moon, I flew into Chicago's O'Hare Airport. It was August 19, 2024, the first day of the Democratic National Convention. Later that morning, I set out to retrieve my press credentials. The Hyatt Regency at McCormick Place, where credentials were kept, was encircled by an enormous security *cordon sanitaire*. Miles of steel fencing and cement barricades, manned by yellow-jacketed Chicago Police and black-clad Secret Service agents, snaked around the Hyatt and the belly of the beast, the United Center, where Democrats from around the country were converging to make Kamala Harris their presidential nominee.

Security was a nightmare—but it was all designed to prevent a repetition of what happened here fifty-six years earlier: the bloodiest and most tumultuous political gathering in modern history, the Democratic Convention of 1968.

Twentieth-century Chicago was a fitting location for the dystopian drama that took place that year—which ended with blood flowing in the streets and the Democratic Party's electoral prospects in ruins. It was a violent, days-long brawl between brutal, baton-wielding cops and National Guardsmen and long-haired hippies, Yippies, and protesters against the Vietnam war; the press corps got swept up in the fray. Pitched battles between cops and protesters took place within a stone's throw of the city's infamous stockyards, where the stench of animal slaughter wafted over the proceedings and mingled with the scent of tear gas.

The streets of Chicago were a battleground. Norman Mailer, the pugnacious author of the World War II novel *The Naked and the Dead,* described the scene from the nineteenth floor of the Conrad Hilton Hotel, where the Democratic nominee Hubert Humphrey was staying: "Children, and youths, and middle-aged men and women were being pounded and clubbed and gassed and beaten, hunted and driven, sent scattering in all directions by teams of policemen who had exploded out of their restraints like the bursting of a boil."

Miraculously, no one was killed. It was a showdown between two halves of a divided nation—liberal opponents of the war and a president who refused to end it versus conservatives who resented elite college kids who seemed willing to let others do the fighting and dying in Vietnam.

It seemed fair to wonder if the outrage inspired by Israel's bloody siege of Gaza in 2024 would match the bitter passions aroused by the Vietnam War in 1968. Since Israel's invasion of the territory in response to the October 7, 2023, attack by Hamas, American college campuses had been engulfed in protest. In Gaza, tens of thousands of civilians had been killed and much of the population was starving. Harris had called for a ceasefire but hadn't repudiated Biden's willingness to supply arms to Israel. Her nuanced approach hadn't mollified opponents of Israel's war machine; on the contrary, it enraged Muslim-American communities across the country. Thousands of protesters, bused in from Minnesota, Michigan, Indiana, Wisconsin, and beyond, were descending on Chicago.

"The country is nothing like it was in 1968," Bill Daley told me on a Zoom call. Son of the city's legendary mayor Richard Daley, who ran Chicago's powerful political machine in the 1960s, Bill, twenty years old at the time, had witnessed the mayhem at his father's side. "Somebody who analogizes what's going on now didn't live through 'sixty-eight," he said.

Maybe—but Americans seemed almost as bitterly divided in 2024. They'd endured nearly ten years of social and political upheaval: cultural warfare, growing income inequality, a bloody attempted insurrection, a lethal pandemic, the abdication of a president, a near-assassination, and a grinding, U.S.-subsidized war that had killed more than 40,000 Palestinian civilians in Gaza. (By 1968, the U.S. had lost 25,000 troops in Vietnam.) All of this was magnified and exacerbated by social media, which didn't exist in 1968.

Like Hubert Humphrey, the Democratic nominee who'd been saddled with Lyndon Johnson's Vietnam War, Kamala Harris was yoked to Biden's complicity in Israel's war on Gaza. The potential for violence during protests at Chicago's 2024 DNC seemed real.

Daley, who'd gone on to become Bill Clinton's commerce secretary and Barack Obama's second White House chief of staff, conceded that there would be trouble. "There'll be good crowds," he said of the expected protests. "Ten thousand people today is a massive amount that can cause a lot of disruption in the street. But they're not going to get anywhere near the United Center. I don't care what they do. That's not going to happen."

• • •

UNCHARTED

As I approached the Hyatt on the morning of my arrival, I introduced myself to three men dressed in black; they turned out to be chaplains of the U.S. Secret Service. "We're here to offer support and comfort if needed," one of them explained. The chaplains insisted that I follow them and whisked me through a magnetometer and screening machine in a tent just outside the United Center. I was now, without a credential, inside the center's security perimeter. This unintended breach of security was corrected at the next checkpoint—when a DNC official politely pointed me toward the exit. Soon I was back out on the street, outside the security perimeter, in search of my credentials.

Throughout the week, delays and searches were the norm. Getting to the United Center meant walking a mile and a half from the first checkpoint. (Enterprising women wore sneakers and pulled out their heels when they arrived.) And yet no one except a few disgruntled journalists and high-end donors seemed to mind. The excitement over Harris's imminent nomination was palpable. Just two months earlier, Democrats had been staring at almost certain defeat with an octogenarian nominee. Now, with a charismatic Black and Asian woman at the helm, victory seemed possible. Security hassles couldn't dampen the enthusiasm of five thousand delegates—Black, brown, white, Asian, AAPI, and predominantly female—who'd been waiting for this day since Hillary Clinton's defeat in 2016.

In 2024, as in 1968, the first order of business at the convention was bidding farewell to the president. Day One would culminate with the evening appearance of Joe Biden, reluctantly stepping aside after an extraordinary intraparty revolt ended his fifty-year career. Properly staging his farewell presented a challenge. How would the party show him respect while not upstaging Kamala Harris, the nominee? Arranging Biden's graceful exit would be tricky—but not as fraught as bidding farewell to Lyndon Johnson had been.

From the first gavel at the '68 convention, rumors had swirled that despite his declared withdrawal from the race, LBJ would swoop in and claim the nomination. (A heliport was built on the Chicago amphitheater just for that possibility.) Johnson loyalists controlled the convention. The party bosses were still in charge. Anything could have happened—especially if Richard Daley, the Democrats' *capo di tutti capi*, wanted it to happen.

Daley was a Johnson ally, but his heart belonged to the Kennedys—and he nearly made Teddy, 36, the nominee. On the third day of the convention, Daley ducked into his trailer just behind the convention podium. He picked up the phone and called one of Kennedy's advisers. "Is he in or out?" Daley asked. There was a pause. "Okay," he said. Daley turned to his son Bill. "Teddy's out," he told him. "We're going with Humphrey."

And so ended Ted Kennedy's best chance of becoming president. (After his 1969 accident at Chappaquiddick Island, Massachusetts, in which a young woman drowned in the backseat of his car, Kennedy probably never had a chance in his ill-fated 1980 campaign against incumbent Jimmy Carter.) In 1968, Hubert Humphrey became the nominee—and went on to lose a heartbreakingly close race to Republican Richard Nixon.

Those days when party bosses picked the nominees were long over. In the twenty-first century, the closest thing to Richard Daley was Speaker Emerita Nancy Pelosi.

• • •

JOE BIDEN'S FAREWELL WOULD PROVE TO BE MORE GRACEFUL than LBJ's. But it, too, would be a challenge; among the Democrats in Chicago, enthusiasm for Harris dwarfed affection for her boss.

In the *New York Times Magazine*, on August 18, Robert Draper wrote, "In the short weeks that could be called the Biden abdication, amid the swelling energy and excitement for his vice president—the rapturous rallies, the explosion of new voter registrations and the rising tide of polls and donations, even a 'White Dudes for Harris' Zoom call—there had to be a sting for Biden, still the sitting president but now watching from the sidelines as she enjoyed an outpouring he never had."

On the convention's first day, the outpouring of excitement for Harris was expertly harnessed and choreographed. At 9:10 p.m. Eastern Time, Beyoncé's "Freedom" started booming from the arena's sound system. Then, without warning or any prior announcement, Kamala Harris strode onto the stage. The crowd, caught by surprise, roared with delight. Harris beamed and waved. The timing was exquisite. The pacing perfect.

This was no accident; nearly every aspect of the convention— from Harris's surprise appearance to her supporting speakers to the musical acts—had been produced with help from Steven Spielberg and Jeffrey Katzenberg. They acted as unpaid advisers to Stephanie Cutter and Minyon Moore, Democratic campaign operatives who planned and ran the event. Former ABC News president James Goldston and his team, who produced the January 6 House Select Committee's video clips, also pitched in—creating short, crisp presentations on subjects ranging from reproductive rights to gun control.

Day One of the DNC celebrated not just Harris but a gaggle of other female stars. Next up, at 9:36 p.m., was Alexandria Ocasio-Cortez, the Democratic congresswoman from New York, and telegenic member of the so-called Squad. After thanking Biden for his service and praising Harris, AOC, the Republican bête noire, went after Trump:

"We know that Donald Trump would sell this country for a dollar if it meant lining his own pockets and greasing the palms of his Wall Street friends. And I, for one, am tired of hearing about how a two-bit union buster thinks of himself as more of a patriot than the woman who fights every single day to lift working people out from under the boots of greed, treading on our way of life."

It was a stem-winding performance, greeted with loud applause. And yet AOC's speech turned out to be just a warmup for an even more electrifying act.

Just before 10 p.m., Hillary Rodham Clinton took the stage. The sight of her sent the audience into a frenzy. After several minutes of foot-stomping, roaring applause, Ms. Clinton stepped up to the podium. It was eight years since her ill-starred run for the presidency, and 104 years and a day since the passage of the Nineteenth Amendment granting women the right to vote. Looking more relaxed than she'd ever been on the stump in 2016, Ms. Clinton declared above the din, "Wow. There's a lot of energy in this room. Just like there is across the country. Something is happening in America. . . ."

Hillary lauded Democratic trailblazers Shirley Chisholm, the Black congresswoman who ran for president in 1972, and Geraldine Ferraro, who became the first female vice-presidential candidate for a major party in 1984. Then she pivoted to her own story: "It was the honor of my life to accept our party's nomination for president—and nearly sixty-six million Americans voted for a future where there are no ceilings on our dreams. And afterwards we refused to give up on America. Millions marched, many ran for office, we kept our eyes on the future. Well, my friends, the future is here!"

Then Hillary turned to Trump, citing his thirty-four felony convictions for falsifying business records in paying hush money to a porn star. The convention broke into a rhythmic cry: "Lock him up! Lock him up!" ("Lock *her* up!" had been the GOP's rallying cry at their 2016 convention.) As the chant continued, the former candidate nodded and smiled.

When she was through, there was such exuberant celebration that I half-expected a "Draft Hillary" campaign to break out on the convention floor. But Hillary's appearance, however galvanizing, was also an uncomfortable reminder of what can happen to a female nominee whose victory had once seemed inevitable.

The program was running late; it was 11:26 p.m. on the East Coast, well past prime time, when the first night's guest of honor finally appeared. Joe Biden was introduced by his 43-year-old daughter, Ashley, as Kamala Harris and second gentleman Doug Emhoff looked on from a box across the arena. To chants of "Thank you, Joe!" Biden began, his voice hoarse but strong, by invoking the victory of democracy over "the oldest forces" in Charlottesville—the hate-filled, neo-Nazi rally that had compelled him to run in 2020. The president lauded a country "where everyone has a fair shot and hate has no safe harbor." Biden spoke about the achievements of his presidency—from passing bipartisan legislation to creating manufacturing jobs to launching infrastructure projects to advancing clean energy. But the recitation landed with a thud, like a laundry list. Even as he prepared to leave the world stage, Biden and his speechwriters still hadn't figured out how to sell his agenda.

"THIS COUNTRY IS NOTHING LIKE IT WAS IN 1968."

The cloud of the Gaza War hung over the proceedings. Convention organizers had turned down a request to allow a Palestinian speaker to address the delegates. But the war still intruded. Hours before Biden made his appearance, protesters had broken through a barricade outside the United Center; the cops had pushed them back. Now the president addressed the issue. "Those protesters out in the street, they have a point," he said. "A lot of innocent people are being killed." Biden vowed to work around the clock to end the war and bring home the Israeli and American hostages, still being held in horrible conditions by Hamas.

It was past midnight; much of Biden's television audience had gone to bed and the crowd was attentive but restless. "It's been the honor of my lifetime to serve as your president," he said. "I love my job, but I love my country more. And all this talk that I'm angry at all those people who said I should step down, it's not true." The arena erupted one last time, chanting, "We love Joe!" Biden closed by reciting lyrics from the song "American Anthem": "Let me know in my heart when my days are through. America, America, I gave my best to you."

After hours of standing on the crowded convention floor, I found an empty seat in the New York delegation. I noticed Letitia James, the state's attorney general, who'd won a $450 million civil fraud judgment against Trump, and Kathy Hochul, New York's governor, sitting together nearby. Then a woman in the California delegation caught my eye. Elegant in a yellow dress, she sat pensively, holding a bright red sign with bold white lettering: "Thank you, Joe." It was Nancy Pelosi.

The next day I texted Manafort.

What's your take on DNC Day One?

UNCHARTED

Not a good night. Dissonance between B-H [Biden-Harris] undercurrent. Plus Hillary a negative.

Then he added:

Got the past out of the way. That was the one good thing. Tonight should be a better night for them.

I replied:

Don't know how it played on TV but the energy here was off the charts. But as Alan Greenspan once said, beware irrational exuberance.

Manafort replied:

The arena is the least important barometer.

What he meant, of course, was that the television audience was the only thing that mattered. I wondered why the Democrats' marquee speakers were scheduled so late in prime time.

But as the Democrats celebrated their new nominee, Donald Trump's campaign seemed to be careening off the track.

While Harris and her supporters stuck to their script in Chicago, Trump was going rogue. This had been happening on a regular basis since Biden dropped out and Harris had replaced him on the ticket. Trump was still furious that he was no longer running against Biden—and he blamed Susie Wiles and Chris LaCivita for scheduling the June debate, which had driven Biden from the race.

Now, on the campaign trail, he was lashing out, veering off script. On July 31, appearing at the National Association of Black Journalists convention in Chicago, Trump claimed that Harris, the daughter of a Jamaican father and Asian mother, had concealed her Black heritage until recently. In fact, she'd proudly cited her membership in AKA, Alpha Kappa Alpha, a Black sorority at Howard University. Trump didn't care. "I didn't know she was Black until a number of years ago when she happened to turn Black and now she wants to be known as Black," he said. "So, I don't know, is she Indian or is she Black?"

Trump's crude performance at the NABJ convention was just the beginning of a barrage of insults fired at Harris. In the weeks that followed, Trump called her a "shit vice president," a "communist," "dumber than hell," "mentally disabled," "low IQ," and "lazy," a racist trope. And just when it appeared that he couldn't sink any lower, on August 28 Trump reposted on his Truth Social account a photo of Hillary Clinton, with the comment: "Funny how blow jobs impacted both their careers differently." This evidently was an insinuation that Harris had traded oral sex for advancement during her career in San Francisco.

During their occasional phone calls, Kellyanne Conway tried to persuade Trump to treat Harris with more respect. Not because it was the right thing to do (never a strong argument with Trump) but because it would be more effective. "In 2016, you treated Hillary like she was a worthy opponent," she told him. "You've got to treat Kamala Harris like she's a worthy opponent."

Trump pushed back, angry about the fact that he'd spent millions running against her predecessor. "Well, they cheated," he said. "We spent $100 million against Biden."

Conway replied: "Absolutely. You are completely 1,000 percent correct. However, nobody's going to care."

But while Trump flailed on the stump, his campaign was readying a barrage of television commercials to be unleashed after the Democrats' convention ended. One of them featured video of Harris expressing her support for funding transgender operations for incarcerated immigrants. It ended with a tag line: "Kamala is for they/them. President Trump is for you."

On August 20, the second day of the Democratic convention, the party was still going strong. That morning, the typically staid, ceremonial roll call of delegates was transformed into a rollicking celebration, as DJ Cassidy spun a playlist of songs for each state—from Alabama's "Sweet Home Alabama" by Lynyrd Skynyrd to Connecticut's "Signed, Sealed and Delivered" by Stevie Wonder, Iowa's "Celebration" by Kool and the Gang, and Wyoming's "I Gotta Feeling" by the Black Eyed Peas. When it came Georgia's turn, with "Turn Down for What," the rapper Lil Jon danced in the aisle as the arena rocked.

That night, Michelle Obama, the country's most popular Democrat, tried to fill in the blanks of the nominee's story. "My girl, Kamala Harris, is more than ready for this moment," she said. "She is one of the most qualified people ever to seek the office of the presidency. And she is one of the most dignified—a tribute to her mother, to my mother, and to your mother, too. The embodiment of the stories we tell ourselves about this country. Her story is your story. It's my story. It's the story of the vast majority of Americans trying to build a better life."

Then she turned to Trump—his inherited fortune, multiple bankruptcies, gaming of the legal system, and golden escalator:

"We will never benefit from the affirmative action of generational wealth. If we bankrupt the business or choke in a crisis, we don't get a second, third, or fourth chance. If things don't go our way, we don't have the luxury of whining or cheating others to get further ahead. No. We don't get to change the rules, so we always win. If we see a mountain in front of us, we don't expect there to be an escalator waiting to take us to the top. No. We put our heads down. We get to work. In America, we *do* something."

She was followed by the party's most gifted orator, Barack Hussein Obama. "I am feeling hopeful because this convention has always been pretty good to kids with funny names who believe in a country where anything is possible," he said. Obama cited Trump's "constant stream of gripes and grievances that's actually been getting worse now that he is afraid of losing to Kamala." And he mocked Trump's apparent obsession with the size of his crowds and with male genitalia. "There's the childish nicknames, the crazy conspiracy theories, this weird obsession with *crowd* sizes." Obama motioned suggestively with his hands, as though measuring something other than crowds. The crowd roared.

The third day of the DNC was designed to show off Harris's vice-presidential pick, Tim Walz. The homespun governor of Minnesota, a shotgun-toting football coach with left-of-center views, had been a dark-horse choice. The conventional wisdom had been that Josh Shapiro, the Pennsylvania governor, would be a stronger VP pick; he was a formidable campaigner who could help her carry his home state, a critical piece of the electoral college's vaunted "blue wall." But Harris worried that Shapiro, who is Jewish and an outspoken defender of Israel, might send a hawkish signal about her intentions toward Gaza. She liked Walz personally and appreciated his homespun appeal to Joe

Biden's blue-collar working class, a voting bloc Harris desperately needed. Walz was a younger, midwestern "Scranton Joe."

Hillary had played a supporting role in Harris's VP decision. The two women, who'd been on opposite sides during the 2008 Democratic presidential primary (with Harris supporting Obama), had grown close since 2020; Hillary often had Harris over to her house, not far from the Naval Observatory, for potluck suppers with Democratic operatives like Rahm Emanuel and Jen Palmieri. And when Harris decided on Walz, Hillary approved.

In his brief time on the ticket, Walz had presented himself as a plainspoken contrast with his Republican counterpart, the high-falutin' Ivy League–educated J.D. Vance. After Vance criticized women without children as "childless cat ladies," Walz ridiculed him and his boss as "weird." In defense of women's reproductive rights, Walz had a message for Trump and the GOP hardliners: "Mind Your Own Damn Business!"

Walz's appearance at the convention was well received—and it was punctuated by a moving, unscripted moment that drove home his everyman appeal. As he concluded his remarks, Walz's 17-year-old son, Gus, leapt to his feet, pointed at his father, and shouted with pride: "That's my dad!" He was in tears. It was a touching scene of a young man with nonverbal learning and anxiety disorders; it would be replayed countless times on social media.

On the convention's fourth and final night, the arena buzzed with a rumor, whipped up on social media, that the singer Beyoncé would appear in the flesh to kick off the evening. It was not to be, but no one really minded. At 10:45 p.m., Kamala Harris strode onto the stage to a thunderous reception.

When the applause abated, Harris warmed to her theme

about the promise of America, paying tribute to her mother, Shyamala Harris, who'd traveled from India to the United States at the age of 19, and to the "beautiful, working-class neighborhood of firefighters, nurses, and construction workers" in Oakland, California, where she'd grown up. "On behalf of Americans like the people I grew up with—people who work hard, chase their dreams and look out for one another. On behalf of everyone whose story could only be written in the greatest nation on Earth, I accept your nomination to be president of the United States of America."

Harris touched all her bases. She told her personal story, defined herself as a fighter for the middle class, promised to tackle the high price of housing and groceries, pledged to protect healthcare and women's reproductive rights, vowed to revive a bipartisan bill to secure the southern border, warned of Trump's threat to democracy, and showed strength and leadership. "As commander in chief, I will ensure America always has the strongest, most lethal fighting force in the world," she vowed, in a nod to undecided Republicans. (This was the first Democratic convention in memory that was frequently interrupted by the patriotic chant "U.S.A.!") "I will always ensure Israel has the ability to defend itself, because the people of Israel must never again face the horror that a terrorist organization called Hamas caused on October seven, including unspeakable sexual violence and the massacre of young people at a music festival.

"At the same time," she continued, "what has happened in Gaza over the past ten months is devastating." She pledged "to end this war, such that Israel is secure, the hostages are released, the suffering in Gaza ends, and the Palestinian people can realize their right to dignity, security, freedom, and self-determination."

She ended on a forward-looking, upbeat note. "You know,

our opponents in this race are out there every day denigrating America, talking about how terrible everything is. Well, my mother had another lesson she used to teach: Never let anyone tell you who you are. You show them who you are."

It was a sure-footed performance, crafted with speechwriter Adam Frankel. The question was, would any undecided voters be persuaded?

THE MORNING AFTER THE CONVENTION, FROM MY HOTEL LOBBY, I heard the loud bleating of air horns and shouting from a block away. It was the last gasp of Chicago's anti–Gaza War protesters. Two young men wearing kaffiyehs and a woman carrying a Palestinian flag beat drums and chanted: "Democrats, your hands are red, 180,000 dead!" A handful of spectators looked on, along with a half dozen cops.

After a convention in which she'd hit all her marks and avoided a repeat of the debacle of 1968, Kamala Harris, the Democratic presidential nominee, was leaving town with the wind at her back.

"THEY'RE EATING THE DOGS, THEY'RE EATING THE CATS."

In the late summer of 2024, Democrats were daring to imagine Kamala Harris as president of the United States. On August 13, on MSNBC's *The Beat with Ari Melber,* a week *before* the convention, James Carville had said the chances of Harris winning by five percentage points were much better than Trump winning by one and a half. Now, in the wake of a nearly flawless Harris coronation in Chicago, many Democrats allowed themselves to imagine that Harris might re-create the winning coalition assembled by Barack Obama in 2008. After all, Obama's ex-campaign manager, David Plouffe, had joined the team as a senior adviser.

Bringing Plouffe aboard the Harris-Walz campaign was a potentially fraught undertaking. Biden might be gone, but Jen O'Malley Dillon still ran the show. She had worked under Plouffe on Obama's first presidential campaign—but now the shoe was on the other foot and she would make sure it stayed there. O'Malley Dillon had built the campaign from the ground up and wasn't going to let Plouffe usurp her authority. "I don't think they ever had a great relationship, and then they were put into this position of trying to be banded together," said a campaign veteran who worked for both. To be effective, O'Malley Dillon, a creature of Biden World, and Plouffe, brought in by Harris, would have to play nicely. But O'Malley Dillon considered herself first among equals; she was not about to be shunted off to run the ground game while Plouffe whispered in Kamala's ear. As a result, Harris had not one but two chief strategists steering the campaign. That's often a recipe for trouble. And a third senior adviser, Stephanie Cutter, was also jostling for influence.

The real question was: Whose campaign was it anyway? Biden's or Harris's?

A new face, Harris, was at the top of the ticket, but would she have a new message? The challenge, said a member of her inner circle, was "We had to merge who she is, her history, with a whole campaign apparatus that wasn't built for her."

The first priority was to tell her story. "There's a lot of things you can say about Kamala Harris," said one of her senior advisers. "You can talk about the prosecutor. You can talk about being the first woman. You can talk about history breaking. You can talk about qualifications. You can talk about her political acumen, like running a big city. You can talk about a lot of stuff. And we had to figure out what. And what are people missing about her? What do they most want to hear? It had to start in July, August from a baby campaign place."

The Biden campaign pooh-bahs had been cramming. "A lot of the people in leadership on that campaign didn't know her," said a Harris aide. "A lot of them read her book for the first time on, like, July 22." Harris would need to find her own voice—and quickly.

• • •

"THEY'RE EATING THE DOGS, THEY'RE EATING THE CATS."

By any conventional measure, the passing of the torch from Biden to Harris at the Democratic convention had been seamless: the speakers compelling, the message broadly appealing, and the television ratings strong; according to Adweek, the DNC averaged 21.797 million viewers per night compared to the RNC's 19.065 million. And if the public polling was any indication, Harris was in a strong position. *Morning Consult's* tracking of the race on August 26 found that she led Trump nationally, 48 to 44 percent. The polling website also concluded that "it's the Democratic nominee's race to lose, and that would certainly not be the case were Biden still in the race."

A senior Trump campaign adviser conceded that the GOP establishment was worried: "Are Republicans bedwetting? Yeah, they are," he said. "They're calling us every day because they're nervous for two reasons. One, because of the tsunami of media favoring Harris, but also because we're running our campaign in the seven battleground states. And unless you live in those states, you don't see the Trump campaign. But if you live in the seven battleground states, you see our campaign. You're feeling our campaign."

Voters in battleground states were being inundated. On August 17, just before the Democratic convention, the opening salvo had been fired in a barrage of Trump television commercials hammering Harris. The first ad interspersed television news reports with video clips of a beaming Harris.

> *TV news reporter: "The alarming spike in inflation, soaring to its highest level in nearly forty years."*
> *Kamala Harris: "That is called Bidenomics."*
> *TV news anchor: "Gas prices rose again today, reaching a new all-time high . . . We're still dealing with inflation and we've got super-high interest rates at the same time."*

> *Harris: "Bidenomics is working!"*
> *TV anchor: "Two thirds of Americans are just struggling*
> *to make ends meet . . . This comes after Friday's jobs report*
> *showing a spike in unemployment."*
> *Harris: "We are very proud of Bidenomics."*

The ad was misleading; it plucked Harris's remarks out of context, and unfairly portrayed Bidenomics as the cause of almost every economic ill. Never mind that the Biden-Harris administration had pulled the economy back from the brink of a depression, created sixteen million jobs, and brought record low unemployment. But all's fair in love and political campaigning and the commercial's message was potent. Harris appeared to be bragging about the misery she and Joe Biden were inflicting on working-class Americans.

One of Harris's senior advisers conceded: "The Trump campaign did a good job of really just pummeling us on her being California, radical, dangerously liberal, all of those things." "Bidenomics" was just the beginning of a televised assault on Harris. Several TV spots portrayed her as Biden's failed "border czar." That was a job Harris never held; as vice president, she'd been tasked not with policing the border but with helping the "northern triangle" countries—El Salvador, Honduras, and Guatemala—address the root causes of immigration. The Trump ads also falsely asserted that she'd offered "amnesty" to ten million immigrants. But the commercials succeeded vividly in tying Harris to two things voters hated about Biden's presidency: the cost of living and the border crisis. At the convention, Harris had portrayed herself as the candidate of change. "We're not going back!" was her signature chant. But the Trump ads were defining her as a creature of the present, not the future.

"THEY'RE EATING THE DOGS, THEY'RE EATING THE CATS."

All this was just a warm-up for one of the most devastating political attack ads of modern times. Drawing upon footage from Harris's 2019 presidential primary campaign, it featured an inmate convicted of murder who'd been sentenced to life in prison. "Kamala Harris pushed to use tax dollars to pay for his sex change," said the narrator. The ad cut to Harris on camera. "I made sure that they changed the policy," she said, "so that every transgender inmate would have access; the power that I had, I used it in a way that was about pushing forward the movement, frankly, and the agenda."

The ad concluded with this damning narration: "Kamala is for they/them. President Trump is for you."

Airing at least 30,000 times, in a $40 million ad buy targeting football games watched by undecided male voters, "They/Them" set off alarm bells among prominent Democrats. Some remembered all too well what had happened in 2004, when Democratic nominee John Kerry was pummeled by ads denigrating his service as a commander of U.S. Navy swift boats during the Vietnam War. That campaign, created by Chris LaCivita for a PAC that supported George W. Bush, accused Kerry of disgracing his uniform. Kerry's failure to respond to "the Swift Boat Veterans for Truth" ads (his campaign was broke at the time) was thought by many to have cost him a close election against Bush.

Now, in the fall of 2024, some thought "They/Them," if left unaddressed, could be just as damaging to Harris. John Fetterman, Pennsylvania's populist Democratic senator, knew a potential knockout punch when he saw one. "How can you sum up 'woke' in one commercial?" he said. "Try and top that." A prominent former Democratic campaign manager reached out to friends in the Harris campaign. "I remember calling one of them in a panic, saying: 'You guys have to answer this transgender thing—like, what are we doing here?'" he said. "And they were like, 'there is no answer. We're just going to ignore it.'"

In fact, the Harris campaign tested at least a half dozen answers—from pointing out that the transgender policy was the law under Trump to saying that Harris had changed her mind. The most effective response, according to focus groups, was when Harris addressed the topic but then immediately changed the subject. A Harris adviser explained: "The ad that we ended up running the most was 'You may have seen some of these ads about me. Here's the deal: I'm focused on the cost of living, blah, blah, blah.' So you pivot to something else." To many, this seemed like a cop-out. "You cannot let the negative lie," the former Democratic campaign manager told me. "You just can't do that."

PRESIDENTIAL CAMPAIGNS HAVE THREE MAJOR, ATTENTION-getting events—or what strategists call "moments." They are the declaration of candidacy, the convention nomination speech, and the televised debates (possibly four, if you count the VP selection). With two months remaining until the election, there was just one "moment" left in the 2024 campaign: the presidential debate between Harris and Trump. It was scheduled to air on ABC News on September 10. The stakes seemed enormous.

Debating was Harris's wheelhouse; as a senator in congressional hearings, she'd dismantled hostile witnesses; as a veteran prosecutor, she'd confronted predators; and as she famously said in her first rally, she knew her opponent's type. For Trump, the encounter was a chance to define Harris as an ultra-liberal defender of the status quo—before she could define herself.

To prepare for the face-off, Harris and her team huddled in a Pittsburgh hotel. For five days, she drilled in mock sessions; this time, instead of Ron Klain, the team was headed by Karen Dunn, a Democratic attorney and Hillary Clinton campaign veteran. Another Clinton alumnus, Philippe Reines, wearing an ill-fitting suit and a long red tie, replaced Bob Bauer as the stand-in for Trump.

At his golf club in Bedminster, Trump prepared by having "policy time" with Florida congressman Matt Gaetz and Tulsi Gabbard, the former Democratic congresswoman from Hawaii.

On the morning of the debate, I asked Manafort about Trump's state of mind. "Is he still pissed off that he's not debating Joe Biden?" I asked him. "No, he's moved on," Manafort replied. "August wasn't a fun month, but he now sees that our campaign has worked. We've been hammering her with our media and our grassroots operation." After weeks of public polling that showed Harris ahead, Trump's mood had been brightened by a *New York Times*–Siena poll, issued September 8, showing him leading Harris by 48 to 47 percent.

Still, Trump was lashing out wildly on Truth Social. Over the weekend of September 7, he unleashed a wild screed: "WHEN I WIN, those people that CHEATED will be prosecuted to the fullest extent of the law. Those involved in unscrupulous behavior will be sought out, caught, and prosecuted at levels, unfortunately, never seen before in our Country."

Manafort was philosophical about these outbursts. "Weekends are always tough," he said. "But he sees it now—the *New York Times*–Siena poll, the internals, show that voters know Trump's for change. She's for the last four years, and you can't trust her." In the debate, Manafort was confident that Trump wouldn't slip into the bullying mode that had hurt him in his 2020 encounter with Joe Biden, when the then-president, suffering from COVID, raged incoherently at his opponent.

The debate began at 9 p.m. sharp at ABC's studio in Philadelphia; in a confident gesture, Harris strode over to Trump's podium and held out her hand. "Kamala Harris," she said crisply. "Have a good debate." Trump shook her hand and the showdown was joined. The moment that would become infamous followed soon thereafter.

It was the idea of a young right-wing agitator named Alex Bruesewitz. One of J.D. Vance's stable of "Very Online influencers," Bruesewitz had latched on to a rumor that Haitian immigrants in Springfield, Ohio, were stealing and eating pets. Vance loved it. The day before the debate, September 9, the VP nominee posted on X: "Reports now show that people have had their pets abducted and eaten by people who shouldn't be in this country."

There were just two problems with this charge. (1) The vast majority of immigrants in the Springfield area were there legally. And (2) the reports of pet eating were bogus. Trump's advisers hoped he would stay away from this nonsense during the debate.

Twenty-seven minutes into the encounter, during a discussion of Haitian immigrants, Trump declared, "In Springfield, they're eating the dogs, the people that came in, they're eating the cats. They're eating the pets of the people that live there."

The moderator, ABC News's David Muir, interjected that Springfield's city manager said there were no credible reports of immigrants eating pets. But Trump batted away the objection: "Well, I've seen people on television. The people on television say, 'My dog was taken and used for food.'"

Incredulous, Harris started chuckling. "Talk about *extreme*," she said. As absurd as Trump's pet-eating rant was, Harris fumbled the answer: "This is I think one of the reasons why, in this election, I actually have the endorsement of two hundred Republicans who have formerly worked with President Bush,

Mitt Romney, and John McCain, including the endorsement of former Vice President Dick Cheney, and Congressmember Liz Cheney . . . and when we listen to this kind of rhetoric, when the issues that affect the American people are not being addressed, I think the choice is clear in this election."

Harris could have pounded Trump for making up stuff instead of *doing something* about the border—and pointed out that he'd killed a tough bipartisan border security bill that would have helped solve the problem. Instead, she trotted out a list of establishment Republican figures who supported her—a *Who's Who* of the status quo.

Harris was otherwise sharp through the rest of the debate and methodically prosecuted her case. She set various traps that Trump stepped into—from those about the size of his crowds to his felony convictions.

Had it been an Oxford debate, with points for argumentation, evidence, delivery, and rebuttal, Harris would have won it going away. And indeed, afterward, in the spin room, Biden's handlers were gleeful while Trump's were subdued. (Trump himself, glowering, joined them in the room.) Political writers and pundits had a field day at Trump's expense. On September 15, in his *The Best and the Brightest Impolitic* newsletter, the usually spot-on John Heilemann wrote: "the totality of Donald Trump's debate decimation by Kamala Harris was as staggering as it was indisputable."

But Harris's performance was neither staggering nor indisputable. It was true that Trump had repeatedly lied—about immigrants and crime rates and his economic record—and he'd stooped to a new low with his howler about dogs and cats. But outside the chattering classes of the elite media, Trump had effectively defined the choice between him and Harris: change versus more of the same. His closing argument posed a simple question: "So she just started by saying she's going to do this, she's going to do that, she's going to do all these wonderful things," said Trump. "*Why hasn't she done it?* She's been there for three and a half years. They've had three and a half years to fix the border. They've had three and a half years to create jobs and all the things we talked about. *Why hasn't she done it?* . . . We're a failing nation. We're being laughed at all over the world. Wars going on in the Middle East, wars going on with Russia and Ukraine . . ."

Trump appeared to understand something that Harris, for all her debating prowess, did not: The most effective campaign message in the world is "Throw the bums out."

Inside-the-beltway pundits who were appalled by Trump's eating-the-cats-and-dogs gambit were also wrong. To be sure, Trump's claim was not only untrue but arguably racist—and irresponsible: It triggered bomb threats and evacuations at schools in the Springfield area. But far from being politically damaging, Trump's weird tale actually worked; it energized his base—and was a source of amusement, not dismay, for many undecided voters.

The notion of pet-eating immigrants resonated positively among multitudes who didn't care whether it was true. They cared about an invasion of immigrants across the southern border and the dogs-and-cats memes called attention to it. "He actually won the Haitian thing," said Brad Parscale, Trump's 2020 campaign manager. "He made it funny. When Trump entertains, he wins. And so what he did was he converted that cat thing into entertainment."

Sure enough, despite her critically acclaimed debate performance, Harris received no discernible bump in the polls. But there was a bright spot; on the night of the debate, the mega pop star Taylor Swift endorsed Harris's candidacy—and in a swipe at J.D. Vance, she posted a photo of herself on Instagram as a childless cat lady.

THE DAY AFTER THE DEBATE, ON SEPTEMBER 11, TRUMP FLEW TO New York City for a memorial service for the victims of the 9/11 attacks. Aboard Trump Force One, as his staff called his campaign plane, was a surprise guest: Laura Loomer.

Of all the outlandish characters that came and went from Mar-a-Lago, Loomer was possibly the most outrageous and reviled. A right-wing activist, she was infamous for her racist, sexist, homophobic, and Islamophobic views. She described Islam as a "cancer," appeared to applaud the deaths of Mediterranean migrants—and called 9/11 "an inside job" (which made her presence at the World Trade Tower ceremony wildly inappropriate). Moreover, Trump seemed unable to keep his hands off her.

One 2016 Trump campaign veteran thought whoever approved Loomer's seat on Trump's plane should be fired. "I don't know whose fault it is, but they're idiots," she said. (By all accounts, Susie Wiles reluctantly approved Loomer's seat on the campaign plane.) This ex–Trump campaign official was sure the Loomer episode wouldn't end well. "I was very clear about trying to stop the crazies from having a say and giving them any kind of platform with the president. It's suicide to have people like that associated with him. He's surrounded by people now who won't fight him on stuff."

When I asked Lewandowski why Trump liked having Loomer around, he said it was for her skill at "opposition research." In any event, Trump evidently grew tired of whatever it was she offered. Within a few weeks, Loomer was gone. The word was that Trump was appalled by the extent of her plastic surgery.

EVERY PRESIDENTIAL CAMPAIGN DREADS AN OCTOBER SURPRISE. In late September, the Biden White House defused two potential crises that might have derailed Harris's campaign. On September 26, Hurricane Helene made landfall in the southeastern U.S. The storm devastated Georgia and North Carolina, killing 230 and leaving a swath of destruction stretching from northwestern Florida to Tennessee, Georgia, and North Carolina. Biden quickly mobilized the Federal Emergency Management Agency (FEMA) to direct every available asset to the affected areas.

Despite the agency's rapid response, Trump claimed that Biden and Harris were ignoring the natural disaster. On September 27, while campaigning in Valdosta, Georgia, he falsely claimed that the state's governor, Brian Kemp, had been unable to reach the president by phone. Both Biden and Kemp refuted this lie—and although Trump kept repeating it, the political damage was contained. This hurricane was followed, on October 1, by a potential economic disaster—when nationwide dockworkers declared a strike. This would have exacerbated the supply-chain bottlenecks and delays caused by Helene. Biden's White House chief of staff Jeff Zients led a round-the-clock effort to resolve the impasse. At 5:30 a.m. on Thursday, October 3, Zients convened a Zoom call with executives of container shipping lines that had been refusing to budge in talks with the dockworkers. Zients demanded they produce a reasonable offer and told them he was going to brief the president within the hour.

Twelve hours later, White House officials had a deal to reopen the ports until January, postponing the issue until after the election and sparing Harris a major economic and political debacle.

In early October, Harris accepted an invitation to appear on the ABC program *The View*. The show, hosted by Whoopi Goldberg, Sunny Hostin, and four other women, was known for its relatively soft questions and large, predominantly female audience. This was an opportunity for Harris to drive turnout among a crucial demographic group: white women. It would also be a chance to answer a question that was almost certain to come up: Would you do anything differently from Joe Biden?

Sure enough, early in the conversation, on October 8, Hostin asked the question: "Would you have done something differently than President Biden during the past four years?" Harris paused. Then, tentatively, she ventured, "There is not a thing that comes to mind in terms of—and I've been a part of most of the decisions that have had impact."

It was a stunning moment, almost as astonishing as Joe Biden's incoherent answer about Medicare during his debate with Trump. Watching from different corners of the studio were Harris aides Brian Fallon and Kirsten Allen, and Stephanie Cutter, senior adviser on messaging strategy. They were texting each other, "Like, fuck, how do we get her to clean it up?" Harris tried to clean it up a few minutes later by promising to put a Republican in her cabinet. But the damage had been done.

Not only should Harris have had an answer to such an obvious question; it was the question that, more than any other, would define her campaign. A "change candidate" has to explain what kind of change she plans to deliver. But when asked, Harris whiffed; she had no answer at all.

Within twenty-four hours, the Trump campaign had written, produced, and begun airing a new TV commercial. It began with the narration: "A flood of illegals. Skyrocketing prices. Global chaos. And Kamala wouldn't change a thing." Then came the question from *The View*: "Would you have done something differently than President Biden during the past four years?" And Harris's reply: "There is not a thing that comes to mind." The narration concluded: "Nothing will change with Kamala. More weakness. More war. More welfare for illegals. And even more taxes. Only President Trump cut middle-class taxes and only President Trump will do it again."

It was almost inconceivable that Harris's advisers hadn't prepared her for this question. But one Biden campaign veteran wasn't so sure they'd even discussed it. "I could believe a world where they didn't really talk about it." The problem, she said, was "they were so insular to Biden, and that's always been their problem. A lot of people feel like the Biden cabal at the top never talked to anyone else." As a result, she said, "I don't think any of them would ever say, 'Hey, look, the way the withdrawal from Afghanistan went down was wrong. We could have done it better.' I don't think anyone on that team would have had the guts to say that."

If it was any consolation, the next day the Harris-Walz campaign announced that during its short duration, it had raised a billion dollars; by contrast, the Trump campaign had raised $853 million in all of 2024.

In early October, Harris and her team began discussing a possible appearance on a podcast called *The Joe Rogan Experience*. A powerhouse of the right-wing social media universe,

"THEY'RE EATING THE DOGS, THEY'RE EATING THE CATS."

Rogan reached 14.5 million followers on Spotify, almost triple the platform's second most popular program. An Ultimate Fighting Championship commentator, Rogan also reached 19 million followers on Instagram and 17 million on YouTube. On October 25, Trump had appeared on his podcast, at his son Barron's urging, and made thirty-two false claims over three hours, according to CNN. Rogan's most dedicated listeners were male and Black—two demographics with whom Trump had made major inroads and whom Harris was desperate to attract.

But the prospect of Harris appearing on Rogan's show triggered complaints from some of the campaign staff. African-American and progressive staffers thought Harris shouldn't legitimize someone they considered a racist and a toxic peddler of conspiracy theories. Word of this dissension leaked and sparked stories about the Harris campaign's alleged political correctness. Some news outlets got carried away with their indignation; *The National Review* accused the Harris campaign of being "pulled around on a nose-ring by its own staff."

Jennifer Palmieri, who managed second gentleman Doug Emhoff's campaign, would later confirm these reports of infighting to *The Financial Times*. Then she backpedaled, posting on "X" that Harris's failure to do Rogan's show was a matter of logistics: "VP didn't appear on Rogan because of schedule (hard to get to TX twice in a 107 day campaign)." It was true that in the end Harris offered to appear on the podcast if Rogan would meet her on the road—and Rogan declined. In any event, it was a missed opportunity to reach an enormous audience of men—men who were breaking for Trump.

• • •

SINCE THE CONVENTION, HARRIS HAD BEEN TRYING TO WIN OVER conservative Republicans—such as those who'd abandoned Trump for former UN ambassador Nikki Haley. Harris's campaign appearances with ex–GOP congresswoman Liz Cheney were aimed at those centrist anti-Trump Republicans. But "Trump amnesia" was a problem—the inability of some voters to recall just how dysfunctional and chaotic Trump's first term had been. For many, the pre-COVID, pre-inflation years, seen through a gauzy lens, were some sort of golden era. To drive home the danger of a second Trump term, the campaign highlighted just how many of Trump's White House colleagues found him too dangerous to serve another term. On September 22, seven hundred members of the National Security Leaders for America—retired generals, admirals, senior noncommissioned officers, and ambassadors—released a statement endorsing Harris and branding Trump as unfit for the job of commander in chief.

It had been nearly six years since John Kelly, the four-star Marine general, had been fired as Trump's White House chief of staff. Since then, he'd become an outspoken critic of the former president. In a piece for *The Atlantic*, on September 3, 2020, Jeffrey Goldberg reported that during a presidential trip to Paris in 2018, Trump had refused to attend a World War I memorial ceremony at Aisne-Marne American Cemetery because it was "filled with losers." On the same trip, Trump referred to 1,800 Marines who died at Belleau Wood as "suckers." John Kelly had been the source for these stories.

Now, alarmed by the prospect of a second Trump presidency, Kelly was taking another shot at his former commander in chief. For an article in *The New York Times*, on October 22, Kelly agreed to be audiotaped by reporter Michael Schmidt. He confirmed Trump's comments about "suckers and losers" and the ex-president's admiration for Adolf Hitler. Then, consulting a dictionary, Kelly added, "Certainly the former president is in the far-right area, he's certainly an authoritarian, admires people who are dictators—he has said that. So he certainly falls into the general definition of fascist, for sure."

During the campaign, Trump had promised to be a dictator on Day One, vowed to terminate the Constitution and use the military against his domestic opponents. Now, despite having no chance of carrying deep-blue New York State, and with the election just weeks away, Trump was planning to stage a massive campaign rally at New York City's Madison Square Garden. Politically, it made no sense. Why?

It might have been the allure of a famous arena. After all, the Garden had staged the classic 1974 heavyweight championship fight between boxers Muhammed Ali and Joe Frazier. And countless other marquee sporting and cultural events had taken place there.

It also happened to be the site of an infamous Nazi rally, held on February 20, 1939.

"AN ISLAND OF GARBAGE"

A t 3 p.m. on Sunday, October 27, a sunny afternoon, I took the #1 subway train from my home on the Upper West Side to Madison Square Garden in midtown Manhattan. The storied arena, famous for showcasing the world's best athletes, celebrities, and entertainers—from Ali and Frazier to the New York Knicks and the Rangers, to Frank Sinatra, Elton John, and Taylor Swift—was the site of Donald Trump's most anticipated rally of the 2024 campaign. To thousands of MAGA disciples who flocked there, this was a heady celebration of a leader on the verge of a historic political comeback.

To others, it was reminiscent of another event at this same arena eighty-five years before.

On February 20, 1939, six and a half months before Adolf Hitler invaded Poland, more than twenty thousand Americans gathered at the Garden. They gave Nazi salutes to a 30-foot-tall portrait of George Washington flanked by swastikas. The "Pro-American Rally" was the brainchild of Fritz Kuhn, leader of the German American Bund, a fascist organization that supported Hitler's Nazis.

For Trump, who'd been credibly accused of being a fascist

and wished "his generals" would act more like Hitler's, choosing to hold a rally at the site of that Nazi gathering seemed strange. But many things about Trump World were odd to me, and they were about to get odder still.

Outside the Garden, security was tight. I carried a "Special Guest" credential—courtesy, I was told, of Caroline Wiles, the 37-year-old daughter of Trump's campaign manager Susie. Showing the pass, I was waved past the first NYPD sawhorse, where I waited with a half dozen Trump VIPs. After a half hour, we were escorted into the arena, through security screeners, and onto an elevator that took us up to the fifth floor. This was where Trump's friends and donors, behind velvet rope lines, could watch the proceedings while sipping cocktails in VIP suites.

Stepping off the elevator, I nearly collided with a grinning Vivek Ramaswamy, dressed in a dark suit. Right behind him was Rod Blagojevich, the disgraced ex–Democratic governor of Illinois, who served eight years in prison for trying to sell Barack Obama's Senate seat but was pardoned by Trump. Before I could get much farther, someone wearing a lanyard asked to look at my pass. It turned out I wasn't such a special guest after all. She escorted me to an exit, which led out to the main arena.

The Garden was packed; I found an empty seat in the upper, nosebleed section next to a woman named Donna and her 20-something daughter; they'd driven three hours from the Lake George region of New York State to be here. This was their third Trump rally, Donna told me. The others had been in Roxbury, Massachusetts, and on Long Island. "The Long Island rally was really rowdy," she said. "What do you mean?" I asked. "There were fistfights," she said. "In the parking lots—with counterprotesters." There'd been no fights at the Garden so far, but Donna was impressed by the vibe. "This one is really energetic," she said.

It was true. The arena was buzzing with energy, excitement—and anger. Anger at minorities, people of color, Puerto Ricans, transgender athletes, liberal judges, San Franciscans, mainstream media, and the "elites"—Nancy Pelosi, Hillary Clinton, Kamala Harris, AOC, and Tim Walz. (Or "Tampon Tim," as he was known here, for his support of women's reproductive rights.) When I arrived, a comedian named Tony Hinchcliffe, performing on the stage far below us, had just told jokes disparaging Jews, Palestinians, and Blacks carving watermelons. "I don't know if you guys know this," he said, "but there is literally a floating island of garbage in the middle of the ocean right now. I think it's called Puerto Rico."

The crowd laughed. This would become the most talked about slur of the event—perhaps because it could potentially cost Trump votes in the crucial blue-wall state of Pennsylvania, home to 473,000 Puerto Ricans. But it was hardly the only slur, or even the most offensive at this rally, billed as "the closing argument" of Trump's 2024 campaign.

A radio host with a shaved head named Sid Rosenberg followed Hinchcliffe. He was a New Yorker but had returned recently from an overseas trip. "I just got back from Israel about two weeks ago," he said. "Out of character for me to speak at a Nazi rally, I was just in Israel—but I took the gig!" He segued from this awkward joke to MAGA's favorite villain, Hillary Clinton. "She is some *sick bastard*, that Hillary Clinton, huh?" The crowd roared. "What a *sick son of a bitch*—the *whole fucking party*, a bunch of *degenerates*, low lives, Jew haters, and low lives."

What was he talking about? Was Hillary a sex trafficker operating out of a Washington, D.C., pizza parlor? Were Democrats Jew haters? Whatever he meant, the MAGA faithful loved it. Rosenberg sounded one of the event's main themes: "Americans" vs. the other. "You got homeless and veterans—Americans, Americans—sleeping on their own feces on a bench in Central Park," he shouted. "But the *fucking illegals*, they get whatever they want, don't they?!" Another roar went up.

It felt like a contest to see who could own the libs in the most offensive way. David Rem, a New York City sanitation worker, called Harris "the anti-Christ" and "the Devil" while brandishing a crucifix. A businessman named Grant Cardone declared that Harris "and her pimp handlers" would destroy the country.

With each insult the crowd grew more excited. Compared with these speakers, Trump's hardline immigration adviser, Stephen Miller, seemed almost tame. "America is for Americans and Americans only," he declared. But Miller's words were uncannily similar to what the fascist Kuhn had said eighty-five years earlier in the same spot: "We, with American ideals, demand that our government shall be returned to the American people who founded it."

Miller might or might not have been aware of this echo; history was never a strong suit for Trump and his advisers. When the Manhattan real estate mogul first ran for president, he'd never heard of "America First," the isolationist, fascist-sympathizing movement of the 1930s. (Trump did know that Charles Lindbergh, a member of the America First Committee, was a pilot.) But during an interview with Trump in March of 2016, David Sanger of *The New York Times* pointed out similarities between America First and MAGA. Trump soon adopted the slogan as his own.

Being at the Garden that day was like going through the looking glass; in this alternate reality, Harris was a cruel witch and Trump a kind soul. Trump's childhood friend David Rem, who'd been lambasting Hillary Clinton as the Devil, shifted gears and told a touching story; Trump's father, Fred, the real estate developer, had put him and his sisters through school after his father died of a heart attack. "Can you imagine Kam-IL-a Harris performing a kind, generous act like that?" he asked. "Nooooooo!" the crowd roared. I looked over at Donna, my new MAGA acquaintance; she was shaking her head vigorously and clapping as Rem shouted. "Never. Never Ever!"

Donna and her daughter didn't strike me as haters—so what was this about? Not so much the banality as the normality of evil. As Susan Glasser wrote on October 31 in *The New Yorker*: "the nastier the nickname, the cruder the slur, the bigger the roar. The people were not . . . particularly angry, but they were all-in . . . [on] the cult of personality, the calculated hurling of vicious insults, the demonization of entire groups of people. 'Tampon Tim' and Harris's 'pimp handlers' were not regrettable aspects of the rally . . . They were the attraction."

Soon afterward, Rudy Giuliani took the stage. To most New Yorkers, the city's hard-nosed, tough-on-crime mayor of the 1990s, who later became Trump's lawyer, had become a cartoonishly pathetic figure—an addled conspiracy theorist, insurrectionist, election-denier, and bully who'd smeared innocent election workers with bald-faced falsehoods that caused them to live under death threats. (A court had ordered Giuliani to pay plaintiffs Ruby Freeman and Shaye Moss $148 million in damages.) And yet, in this arena, Giuliani was a hero, once and forever "America's mayor," basking in adoration and applause from twenty thousand fans.

There were thirty speakers in all, including Giuliani, the TV personality Dr. Phil, Ultimate Fighting Championship CEO Dana White, anti-vaccination activist Robert F. Kennedy, Jr., ex-Fox News host Tucker Carlson, and billionaire Elon Musk. They painted a dark but evidence-free picture of America: crime was soaring (in fact, it had dropped dramatically); immigrant hordes were invading (in fact, immigrants were crossing the border at a slower rate in October 2024 than during much of Trump's presidency); inflation was skyrocketing (in fact, the inflation rate was declining); manufacturing jobs were vanishing (in fact, 775,000 manufacturing jobs had been created since 2021). Lost on this crowd was the fact that Trump had jettisoned more jobs in his first term than any president since Herbert Hoover. In this arena, it was a given that Trump's economy was the greatest ever until Biden came along and ruined it.

The litany of doom and gloom went on and on. Finally, at 7:13 p.m., Donald Trump took the stage.

To chants of "U.S.A.!" Trump kissed Melania and pumped his right fist in the air. "I'd like to begin by asking a very simple question," he said. "Are you better off now than you were four years ago?" The crowd replied: "Noooooooo!" Trump continued: "I'm here today with a message of hope for all Americans: With your vote in this election, I will end inflation. I will stop the invasion of criminals coming into our country and I will bring back the American dream. Our country will be bigger, bolder, richer, safer, and stronger than ever before."

Trump seemed mild compared to the speakers that preceded him. But he couldn't resist dusting off one of his favorite authoritarian tropes. "We're running against something far bigger than Joe or Kamala and far more powerful than them," he said, "which is a massive, vicious, crooked, radical left machine that runs today's Democrat party . . . they are indeed the enemy within."

Later, Trump would call the event a "lovefest."

The next day, at Joint Base Andrews, Kamala Harris was asked by a reporter what she thought of the rally. Trump, she said, "fans the fuel of hate and division and that's why people are exhausted with him."

But as I left the Garden that night, the place was still packed and no one looked exhausted.

TWO DAYS LATER, KAMALA HARRIS DELIVERED HER CAMPAIGN'S summation. The site she chose was Washington, D.C.'s Ellipse, where, on January 6, 2021, an armed mob stormed the U.S. Capitol after an incendiary speech by Trump. The contrast between the venues said everything about the difference between the candidates: Trump the showman in the world's most famous arena versus Harris the prosecutor at the scene of the crime.

Harris and her advisers had debated which issue to emphasize in her campaign's final stretch: There were plenty, all of them urgent: lowering the cost of living, safeguarding reproductive rights, cracking down on the southern border, and protecting democracy, to name a few. The priority, they decided, should be Trump's existential threat to democracy.

Some Democratic veterans thought this was a weak closing argument. "No one wakes up every day thinking about democracy," said Jennifer Ridder, a former Biden campaign official and chief of staff to Denver mayor Mike Johnston. "I'm sure it polls well. I'm sure people think that democracy is at stake, but they don't think it affects their own lives."

She compared the issue to conservation in the western states. "Preserving public lands always polls the best, as the number one issue. But no one ever votes on it. And the Harris campaign went back to the democracy message at the end. And I was just like, 'Wait, what?' It just seemed very out of touch."

On a crisp Tuesday evening, October 29, Harris addressed her supporters at the Ellipse. Forty thousand people were expected but nearly seventy-five thousand showed up. Framed by American flags, with the White House's South Portico gleaming behind her, Harris made her closing campaign pitch. Until now she'd avoided Biden's soaring rhetoric, often penned by Mike Donilon and historian Jon Meacham; instead of calling for a battle for the soul of the nation, she'd dismissed Trump as a tired circus act. "On Day One, if elected—on Day One, Donald Trump would walk into that office with an enemies list," she said. "When elected, I'll bring a to-do list." Harris promised to do everything on that list: enact a federal ban on grocery price gouging, limit prescription prices, build affordable housing, enact a childcare credit, make Medicare cover home care, restore the protections of *Roe v. Wade*, sign a border security bill, and strengthen America's global leadership.

She finished on a high note. "I pledge to you to approach my work with the joy and optimism that comes with making a difference in people's lives. And I pledge to be a president for all Americans. And to always put country above party and self." Then came a Meacham-esque flourish: "Those who came before us, the patriots at Normandy and Selma, Seneca Falls and Stonewall, on farmlands and factory floors, they did not struggle, sacrifice, and lay down their lives only to see us cede our fundamental freedoms. They didn't do that—only to see us submit to the will of another petty tyrant."

Once again, Harris had touched all her bases. But would anyone be persuaded?

For the moment, Harris's high-minded rhetoric about democracy was eclipsed by Tony Hinchcliffe's racist joke about Puerto Rico being an island of garbage. Two days after the Garden rally, there was genuine outrage. Puerto Rican pop stars Bad Bunny and Ricky Martin denounced the remark and declared their support for Harris. Nicky Jam, a reggaeton singer, announced that he was withdrawing his endorsement of Trump. Political analysts predicted that the slur might cost Trump Pennsylvania, which was home to over 400,000 eligible Puerto Rican voters. But just as the Hinchcliffe contretemps appeared to be giving a boost to the Harris campaign, Joe Biden blundered into the dust-up and turned it into a liability.

On October 29, on a Zoom call with a Latino voters organization, the president said, "The only garbage I see floating out there is his supporter's—his, his, his demonization of Latinos is unconscionable and it's un-American." The garbage Biden was referring to, he later clarified, was Hinchcliffe's "hateful rhetoric." (It all depended on the placement of the apostrophe in "supporters.") But Trump and his advisers insisted Biden was calling his MAGA supporters "garbage." It was, they said, a variation on Hillary Clinton's infamous 2016 crack about Trump's "deplorables."

Chris LaCivita had an idea. Why not drive home Biden's gaffe with a stunt that would keep it alive on television and social media? When Trump arrived in Green Bay, Wisconsin, the next day, a garbage truck, with TRUMP in bold letters on its side, was parked on the tarmac. Wearing a sanitation worker's reflective orange vest, Trump climbed off his plane and walked over to the truck. Then he carefully pulled himself up into the cab—and tooted its horn.

The spectacle was ridiculous—reminiscent of the time when Michael Dukakis, the 1988 Democratic nominee, wearing a helmet that made him look like Snoopy in the *Peanuts* cartoon, climbed into a tank and rode it toward a television camera. Dukakis was mocked—and lost the election to George H.W. Bush. But who knew how Trump's garbage truck stunt might play? The usual laws of campaign politics never seemed to apply to him.

At a rally in North Carolina that same day, Trump declared, "This week, Kamala has been comparing her opponents to the most evil mass murderers in history. And now, speaking on a call from her campaign last night, crooked Joe Biden finally said what he and Kamala really think of our supporters. He called them garbage. No way."

By late October, early voting was well underway; 48 million Americans had voted in forty-seven states. Paul Manafort claimed the early trends were bad for Harris. "We're winning and her vote is underperforming in early voting by about twenty-five percent," he told me. "And it's where you would think—in the urban areas, the Black community, the Hispanic community. The fact that they haven't been able to get out the urban area vote is a bad sign for them."

Manafort said the Biden camp knew this and had adjusted its strategy for the final stretch. "That's why she closed with the fascist, Hitler, stuff," he said. "Because it's meant to motivate any soft potential anti-Trump vote. It's not the Harris vote. It's turning out the anti-Trump vote—which won't show up. And that's their whole game for the close. That's not a reliable strategy, but it's the only one they have."

Manafort compared Harris's race to Hillary Clinton's. "They've run a better strategic campaign than Hillary did. Except she's a more flawed candidate than Hillary. And she's not getting the base vote of a Democratic candidate. With Hillary, people didn't doubt that she could be president. They just didn't want her to be president. But they don't think Harris is up to it. It's that three o'clock in the morning phone call. Harris has not proven her bona fides."

Most of all, Manafort said, Harris was the wrong candidate for voters who wanted change. "If there were a primary today in the Democratic Party to pick a nominee, Harris wouldn't win," he said. "There were other candidates, any one of whom could have been more dangerous for Trump because they weren't tied down by the Biden record. Besides being a bad candidate, her biggest problem is she's tied down to the Biden record. And she can't turn the page, so to speak, with credibility."

Trump's task, Manafort said, was simple. Stick to the message: "She caused it, I'll fix it."

But could Trump stick to that message? As the campaign approached the bell lap, he seemed unmoored. On October 14, at a rally in suburban Philadelphia, two medical emergencies interrupted the proceedings; afterward, instead of returning to his speech, Trump spent forty minutes swaying on the stage to a playlist of his favorite songs as a baffled Kristi Noem, the governor of South Dakota, looked on. On October 19, at a rally in Latrobe, Pennsylvania, hometown of the legendary golfer Arnold Palmer, Trump spent twelve minutes talking about the size of Palmer's genitalia. Then he slammed Harris as "crazy" and added, "You have to tell Kamala Harris that you've had enough, that you just can't take it anymore, you are a shit vice president. The worst."

The Harris campaign's hope was that Trump would say or do something so reckless that it would alienate swing voters in the home stretch. But nothing Trump said seemed to damage him. Back in 1983, Congresswoman Pat Schroeder called Ronald Reagan the "Teflon president" because negative things never stuck to him. But Trump was coated with something more powerful than Teflon; loathsome behavior not only didn't stick, it made him stronger. The worse Trump behaved, the more millions of voters seemed to like him.

Trump had another advantage over Harris—access to a powerful new right-wing echo chamber that bypassed traditional media. The campaign tapped into an online network of influencers and podcast hosts—with names such as the Nelk Boys, Adin Ross, Theo Von, and Bussin' with the Boys. They were unheard of among mainstream audiences but reached millions of young men. These "low-propensity" voters, if mobilized, could make all the difference. Charlie Kirk, executive director of Turning Point USA, a Trump PAC, invested in 350 right-wing influencers, including Benny Johnson, Candace Owens, and Alex Clark. "Win the culture, win the country, that's what we believe," he said.

Harris had missed her chance to reach Joe Rogan's vast audience. And she had nothing comparable to this army of alt-right influencers to spread her message. As David Plouffe would later lament, there was no liberal equivalent to this "well-oiled, invested echo chamber."

PRESIDENTS OFTEN HAVE RICH ALLIES AND CONFIDANTS: FRANKlin Roosevelt confided in railroad magnate Averell Harriman, his ambassador to Moscow; Richard Nixon unwound on Key Biscayne with his friend the wealthy industrialist Bebe Rebozo. But in the history of presidential campaigns, there had never been anything like the relationship between Donald Trump and Elon Musk. Musk, the eccentric South African–born billionaire, initially backed the wrong horse, hosting Ron DeSantis's glitch-filled campaign launch on "X." And Musk hadn't always been a Trump fan; in 2022, he'd tweeted that it was "time for Trump to hang up his hat & sail into the sunset." But now he was the former president's most die-hard fan. Musk had welcomed Trump back on X after he'd been banned from the site following the January 6 attack. Now X, which already promoted pro-Trump content, became his virtual campaign website.

Musk was, of course, the edgy, arrogant plutocrat and entrepreneur who ran Tesla and Space X and was the richest man in the world. *Time* called him a "clown, genius, edgelord, visionary, industrialist, showman, cad . . . the brooding, blue-skinned man-god who invents electric cars and moves to Mars." His companies had revolutionized the manufacturing of electric vehicles and reinvented space flight, sending rockets into space and returning them to land-based silos. Musk and Trump had some things in common: Each believed he was being persecuted by a mythical deep state, and both were addicted to attention.

Musk had been nursing a grudge against Joe Biden and the Democrats ever since the president failed to invite him to a White House conference of electric car makers in August 2021. The White House didn't explain the snub but noted that the other invitees were union companies. Musk was a notorious union buster and enemy of government regulations. But since buying Twitter, he'd taken a darker turn, spouting antigovernment conspiracy theories and going down alt-right rabbit holes. Musk embraced the MAGA gospel, arguing that electing Trump was an existential necessity and that he would be "fucked" if Harris won.

The Trump-Musk bromance was on full display in Butler, Pennsylvania, the scene of Trump's near-assassination, where he returned for a rally to commemorate the event in early October. Introduced admiringly by Trump, Musk, wearing jeans, an "Occupy Mars" shirt, and a dark MAGA cap, bounded onto the stage like a prep school cheerleader before a big game. Images of Musk leaping around the stage bounced around the internet tens of millions of times. "The other side wants to take away your freedom of speech," Musk told the crowd. "They want to take away your right to bear arms. President Trump must win to preserve the Constitution, he must win to preserve democracy in America. This is a must-win situation."

In the final days of the campaign, Musk spent weeks in Pennsylvania, exhorting MAGA voters to get to the polls. But he was more than just a billionaire surrogate; Musk had been put in charge of the campaign's get-out-the-vote effort. The Space X CEO had zero experience at political organizing but was undaunted. He plowed $119 million into a political action committee, America PAC, and recruited veterans of Ron DeSantis's aborted presidential run. (Musk would ultimately sink $280 million into the Trump campaign.)

Rumors of trouble in the Musk ground game began immediately. There were reports that canvassers in Michigan were being driven around in a U-Haul van without seats; many had no idea they were working for the Trump campaign until they signed a nondisclosure agreement. In Arizona and Nevada, canvassers who were paid according to their engagement with voters were reportedly forging 25 percent of their door-knocks. An unnamed

Trump campaign official told *Rolling Stone*, "We never should have outsourced" so much of the ground game operation to that "very strange man."

By contrast, Harris's ground game, run by Jen O'Malley Dillon, was considered the gold standard of presidential campaigns. She'd painstakingly built the operation for more than a year into a state-of-the-art machine—with more than 260 campaign offices and 1,400 staff across the battleground states. They were adding 150 more staff to the Blue Wall states and more than doubling their staff in Arizona and North Carolina.

In a campaign memo on September 1, O'Malley Dillon had noted that Trump's campaign lagged far behind in the infrastructure needed to win the key battleground states. In Nevada, Harris had thirteen offices to Trump's one; in Pennsylvania, thirty-six offices to Trump's three; in Georgia, twenty-four offices to Trump's one. And she added, "While we go on offense to expand our map, the Trump team is on its back foot. In states like North Carolina and Georgia, Team Trump is being forced to spend in ways they did not plan to originally."

Harris's get-out-the-vote effort was a technological marvel, with unprecedented ability to target voters on smart phones, iPads, and almost any other device. A Biden campaign veteran told me that the 2024 Harris campaign was so technologically advanced, it made the 2008 Obama campaign look like something out of the Pleistocene era.

Harris not only had boots on the ground, she had stars on stages. On October 25, the vice president held a rally at the Shell Energy Stadium in Houston, Texas—where she was introduced by Beyoncé, who'd famously failed to show on the last night of the Democratic convention in Chicago. Better late than never. A crowd of thirty thousand, wearing flashing red, white, and blue LED bracelets, had begun gathering before sunrise to see Beyoncé give Harris her endorsement just after 9 p.m.

Although Beyoncé did not sing that night, plenty of A-list musicians did perform at concerts for Harris-Walz: Bon Jovi in Detroit, Christina Aguilera in Las Vegas, Katy Perry in Pittsburgh, Lady Gaga in Philadelphia, and 2 Chainz in Atlanta.

Trump campaign officials were not impressed. "We laughed every time they brought out celebrities," Manafort told me. "All that did is further the divide between the targeted voters we were going after and their base." To the Trump faithful, the conga line of Beyoncé and J Lo merely underscored Harris's image as a candidate of the elites. "It wasn't going to change any workingman's vote in southwestern Pennsylvania," said Manafort.

For all the excitement surrounding Harris, little had changed, in the Trump campaign's view, since Biden's departure. "Look, the race has changed," Manafort told me on October 31, five days before the election. "It's a slightly different race, meaning that Biden had zero chances to win. Harris has one chance to win. We had eight or nine. We have four or five now."

"What's Harris's one chance to win?" I asked him.

"The blue wall and Omaha," he said. The "blue wall" states were Pennsylvania, Michigan, and Wisconsin. "Omaha" was shorthand for the three electoral votes awarded according to Omaha's congressional districts. Nebraska, along with Maine, awarded some of its delegates this way; the other forty-eight states had a winner-take-all formula.

Manafort continued: "That gets Harris to 270. That's her one chance. She's not going to win any of what we call Sunbelt states. We're going to win those four states. And we have to win one of the blue wall. And so we feel good about our chances."

CHAPTER 10

"YOU CAN'T TALK PEOPLE
OUT OF THAT FEELING."

A s the 2024 presidential campaign hurtled toward its conclusion, Harris and Trump crisscrossed the battleground
states. It was an all-out scramble to gain a final edge in the
closest presidential race in modern history.

Trump acted as though he was running scared. Speaking at
Lancaster Airport in Lititz, Pennsylvania, on Sunday, November 3,
he declared he "shouldn't have left" the White House after losing the 2020 election. Later that day, he attacked Democrats as
"demonic" and mused about reporters being in the line of fire in
a future assassination attempt. "To get to me, somebody would
have to shoot through the fake news, and I don't mind that much
'cause I don't mind, I don't mind." As he rambled on, Susie Wiles
made a rare appearance at the edge of the stage—like a headmis-
tress glowering at a misbehaving student.

But while Trump himself was flailing, his campaign was
finishing strong. Wiles and LaCivita had chosen to drive home
the pain people were feeling in the grocery store and at the gas
pump; the "Bidenomics" commercial ran nonstop in the battle-

ground states. To counteract Harris's attacks on Trump's fitness to be president, the campaign also unveiled, for the first time, a positive ad, a sappy paean to Trump's love for America.

The Harris campaign had no comparable closing salvo of paid media advertising. It had sunk most of its remaining money into its get-out-the-vote ground game—after spending $20 million on celebrity concerts; O'Malley Dillon had reportedly delayed signing off on the gigs, driving up the cost.

On the last Sunday before the election, the vice president visited the Greater Emmanuel Institutional Church of God in Christ, in Detroit, Michigan. Taking the podium to cries of "Hallelujah," Harris declared, "In just two days we have the power to decide the fate of our nation for generations to come." After first quoting the prophet Jeremiah, she pivoted to Martin Luther King, Jr.: "I see a nation . . . ready to bend the arc of history toward justice." She was sounding a lot like Barack Obama. That might not have been surprising—since O'Malley Dillon, Cutter, and Plouffe were all veterans of his 2008 campaign. But Kamala Harris was not Barack Obama. She could not match his mastery of hope and change.

The Harris campaign's final days were focused primarily on two themes: preserving abortion rights and protecting democracy. Those issues had been potent in the 2022 midterm elections, but presidential races are different animals. This seemed lost on Harris's team—including Jen O'Malley Dillon. "Look, Jen is brilliant," said a former Democratic presidential campaign manager. "I love her—but they just decided to run the same Biden campaign. And that's not meeting the moment." I spoke to this former-campaign manager three weeks after the election— but he'd tried to sound the alarm to the Harris team in real time. Two thirds of Americans believed the country was on the wrong track. "If that's true," he said, "and if we knew we were losing, why did we make it about abortion? Why did we make it about democracy? They're just running Biden. I don't see how that gets you there with swing voters. Where was the economic message? Where was, 'Hey, I know you're hurting out there.'"

In the campaign's home stretch, the challenge was the same as at the starting gate 107 days earlier: Was it Harris's campaign or Biden's?

Harris's advisers understood the riptide they were swimming against. "All across the world, the change candidate is the one who is winning," said one of them. "So I think that the closing argument was really about charting a path forward that is more optimistic and less hateful and less extreme and all of those things." The campaign was betting on joy over anger. "We felt it was important to close with enthusiasm and optimism and looking forward because what people want is a change election, not going back to two candidates who have already been president, right? Who's going to be the change candidate?"

But to represent change, Harris had to do more than play the Happy Warrior to Trump's monster. It was still Biden's campaign—with its reliance on knocking on doors instead of driving a new message. "It was this huge bet on the ground," said a prominent former Democratic campaign manager. "And they were getting outspent on TV. And that was unfortunate because narrative really matters here."

"Part of what was wrong this time," he continued, "was the whole theory that Trump couldn't win because Trump's so terrible. We've got to stop relying on Donald Trump to suck and actually get our shit together." Biden, not Trump, was the incumbent—and Harris needed to separate herself from him. She and her team still had not tackled this problem head-on.

It wasn't as if they hadn't tried. In October, O'Malley Dillon and Lorraine Voles, Harris's chief of staff, had gone to the White House to tell Jeff Zients, Biden's White House chief of staff, that Harris needed to break with the president—and, in effect, ask him for permission. As one aide put it, "to say, you know, she's got to do this because we've got to win. And they were all like, 'Yeah, do whatever you have to fucking do to win!'" Not only had Zients given the Harris team his blessing, but in a phone call Biden himself told Harris that she should do whatever she had to do, say whatever she wanted to say—his feelings wouldn't be hurt.

Harris and her team struggled with how to do that. After the vice president's flubbed response to that pivotal question on *The View*, she and her team met to brainstorm how to correct it. "I remember distinctly, we were prepping for it," said a senior adviser. "David [Plouffe] saw this from the outset: You have to have a clean break from the president. And it has to be body language as well as words. And so we were going back and forth. And we gave her a recommendation. She didn't take it. And so we did a practice. And we finally landed on like, 'Ma'am, you just, you have to say, my presidency will not be a continuation of Joe Biden's. And we just have to rip the band-aid off.'"

But Harris never did. Saying she wouldn't be a continuation of the Biden presidency wasn't enough. Harris needed to admit that inflation was a scourge and propose a plan to tame it. (Democrats were torn on the issue of the war in Gaza and it was too late for Harris to brand herself as tough on the border.) But Harris was unwilling to buck Biden. Part of it was personal. "There was a hesitancy on her part," said one of her inner circle. "A big, big piece of who Kamala Harris is, is loyal. The reason she's in this position is Joe Biden picked her as vice president and he elevated her after he dropped out. And so there is an element of, like, you dance with the person who brought you."

But it wasn't just Harris who found it difficult to break with Biden; O'Malley Dillon and her deputies were creatures of Biden World and believed in his agenda.

His achievements were their achievements, too. "There was a hesitancy because the things we were running on were successful things, they were popular things," said a Harris adviser. They couldn't believe voters didn't like his policies—they must be unhappy with him. "While what we've done as an administration has been fucking incredible and historic," she explained, "because his name is attached to them, people don't like it." But that wasn't really true; voters didn't hate the economy because it was called "Bidenomics." They hated it because they were struggling to make ends meet. Harris needed to speak to them.

The more I pressed Harris's advisers about her refusal to break with the president, the more excuses I heard. There was the press-will-kill-us argument: If you disagreed with the president, why didn't you argue with him at the time? There was the misogyny argument: A woman will come off as ambitious and conniving if she disagrees with the president. There was even a historical argument: "When in history has a vice president notably broken with their president?" one of Harris's aides asked me. Well, I pointed out, late in his 1968 presidential campaign, Hubert Humphrey broke with Lyndon Johnson on his conduct of the Vietnam War— and almost won the election; his speech in Salt Lake City, Utah, on September 30, 1968, angered LBJ but sparked a surge that almost closed the gap with Republican Richard Nixon. (Humphrey still fell short in a whisker-close election.) The aide countered: "The most notable one in my lifetime was Pence. And that was when fucking Trump told his supporters to hang him!"

If Harris's closest advisers couldn't make this case, why hadn't David Plouffe, the outsider, who was presumably brought in to deliver tough advice? The answer seemed to be that Plouffe, who hated confrontation, was reluctant to force the issue with Harris and O'Malley Dillon. One former Democratic presidential campaign manager said he got calls from Harris staffers who complained about Plouffe's timidity. "All these kids called me and said, 'We thought Plouffe would come in and overrule all these terrible ideas and give us a message. And he doesn't want to fight with her.'" This ex–campaign manager called Plouffe to press the issue, to no avail. "I called him and he's like, 'That's not my role.'"

THE DAY BEFORE THE ELECTION, ALL EYES TURNED TO PENNSYL-vania. Surely O'Malley Dillon's legendary ground operation would out-organize and out-hustle the rookie operation run by Charlie Kirk, head of the Trump PAC Turning Point USA, and Elon Musk. But it turned out that the Trump campaign was reaching persuadable voters in new and innovative ways.

There was a whole untapped world of young men out there— white, Black, and Latino—who were hard to find by knocking on doors but were connected on social media. The Harris campaign knew those voters were out there but struggled to connect with them.

"There was this big group of people who voted for Trump in 2020 and then Democrats in 2022," said an adviser, "hundreds of thousands of those people just in Pennsylvania." Even more important, she said, were the disengaged young voters. "Some of them were like the Black and Latino voters who have moved away from Democrats. Some were white voters who are not engaged either. It is the disengaged voters who we are trying to reach. But they are the hardest to reach." Yet Trump was reaching them—not just through right-wing podcasters and influencers but through apps such as TikTok and Instagram. Trump played to their economic fears and their machismo. "Those people really broke away from us," said the adviser. "We saw that all summer long."

Still, as election day approached, the Harris campaign was projecting confidence and swagger. Appearing on Jen Psaki's MSNBC show back on October 27, O'Malley Dillon had declared, "We are very confident that we're going to win this thing." On Friday, November 1, David Plouffe posted on X that late-breaking undecided voters were breaking for Harris by more than 10 points: "It's helpful, from experience, to be closing a Presidential campaign with late deciding voters breaking by double digits to you and the remaining undecideds looking more friendly to you than your opponent."

That evening, at a dinner for major Democratic donors, top campaign and DNC officials assured them that victory was at hand. Jennifer Palmieri, the Hillary Clinton campaign veteran who was running Doug Emhoff's campaign, had awakened on election day morning in 2016 with a dark sense of foreboding. Now Palmieri allowed herself to believe that Harris would succeed where Clinton had failed.

But warning lights were flashing. Some of Harris's pollsters were baffled by the campaign's happy talk. One Biden campaign veteran told me, "Everyone was willing themselves to the fact that they were going to win. And I was like, 'Well, we're down in every state still.'" Jeff Pollock, one of the Harris campaign pollsters, thought the picture was bleaker than anyone was letting on. He buttonholed a Biden campaign veteran: "What are they talking about?" he complained. "No one is admitting that they might lose," said another former Biden campaign operative. "It was like, is anyone listening—or are we just going to pretend that this is all going to be great?"

Jennifer Ridder, the former Biden campaign official, couldn't understand all the heady talk. "They still had consistent polling results that showed her down by two in every state," she said, "and Trump always overperforms polling. So how the hell were they going to make that up?" Jim Messina, Obama's 2012 campaign manager, didn't get it, either. He went on Psaki's show on Sunday, November 3, and sounded a note of realism. The early voting, he warned, was scary. Turnout was higher than expected in rural areas, favoring Trump, and lower than expected in urban ones, favoring Harris.

In private, Messina hadn't pulled his punches with senior Harris advisers; when he disagreed with their strategy or tactics, he told them, but in public he'd been scrupulously supportive of the campaign. Yet after his comments on Psaki's show, Stephanie Cutter went ballistic, lambasting Messina to Democratic insiders: Why the fuck was he badmouthing the campaign? Word of her outburst got around. It was the same hubris and thin-skinned defensiveness that had been a hallmark of the Biden-Harris campaign from the beginning—when they went after anyone who dared suggest that the president might be too old.

And yet the race was still unpredictable. Voters could break for one candidate or the other. Given the historical tendency of voters to swing one way or the other in the closing days, some political analysts thought both Trump and Harris stood a chance of sweeping all seven battleground states.

A senior Harris adviser was swept up in the excitement of the final sprint. "The closing argument was about the future and the vision for the future, and it felt great," she said. "Everywhere we went, we were getting huge crowds. We were getting a lot of enthusiasm. Every time we saw a governor that last few days, they'd be like, 'No, we're good. It feels good. We got this.' It felt like we were closing strong and that we would win."

On November 3, Ann Selzer, renowned for her solid predictions, forecast that Harris would win Iowa by three points—a state Trump had won by 8 in 2020. "I got thrown a bit by that Iowa poll," said the adviser, "not because I thought it was correct—I didn't. But I thought maybe it was picking up an independent suburban vote that we hadn't quite captured. So it gave a little bit of a false positive there, you know?" Her optimism was reinforced by the throngs of Harris supporters who were turning out at rallies in the final hours. "We were in Philly the night before and had 30,000 people!"

A winning campaign has a gravitational pull, and Lorraine Voles, Harris's chief of staff, was feeling it, too. "You get sucked into the momentum," she said. "Like you believe it. I really thought we were going to win. I thought it was going to be tight because Jen [O'Malley Dillon] kept telling us it was in our morning meetings. She always emphasized how tight it was—up one, down one, up this or that. But she thought we were going to win, too. I've been on winning ones and losing ones and this felt more like Clinton than Dukakis. The rallies were so big and so enthusiastic. And people would wait for so long and it wasn't easy, they were lining the streets." Voles wasn't talking poll numbers or analytics but intangibles. "It just felt really good," she said.

On election morning, at the Naval Observatory, Kamala Harris gathered with her family in the front of the house. Sheila Nix, her campaign chief of staff, Voles, and others were in the back, monitoring returns. Jen O'Malley Dillon; Brian Fallon, the VP's senior aide; Michael Tyler, the campaign communications director; and Quentin Fulks, deputy campaign manager, were running the campaign nerve center at the Marriott Marquis hotel near Howard University, with an army of data crunchers. O'Malley Dillon kept Harris and her team informed as returns came in.

At first the trends were mixed. "We were hearing things like, 'The Philly turnout looks good, but the Atlanta suburbs don't,'" said Voles. After a few hours in the chaotic, cramped quarters of the back office, Voles, Nix, Kirsten Allen, and Ike Irby, another aide, decided to get some air. "We went and sat in my car so we could all talk and call people and find out what was going on," she said.

The vice president was lying low with her family. "We saw her maybe one time that whole night; she came back," said one of her inner circle. As the evening wore on, "It was just like, 'What's going on?' The SG [Second Gentleman] would come in. Doug would say, 'What's happening?'" The realization grew that it was going to be a difficult night.

Over at the White House, on the second floor of the residence, Joe Biden was hosting a large group of advisers, friends, and their spouses. At first, everyone mingled and dug into a spread of Italian food. Most of Biden World was there: Annie Tomasini, Anthony Bernal, Zients, Ricchetti, Donilon, Bruce Reed, political director Emmy Ruiz, his personal secretary Julia Reed, deputy chief of staff Natalie Quillian, and Biden's granddaughters Naomi and Finnegan. Ron Klain was there, too.

As the returns came in, the mood grew glum. "The public reporting was not that optimistic," said Klain. "The *New York Times* needle was at eighty-eight percent for Trump at that point. And the public analysis on TV that we were watching was very negative. So the bad news did not, sadly, surprise him." But the president kept a stiff upper lip. He called Angela Alsobrooks, the newly elected Democratic senator from Maryland, to congratulate her on her victory.

Sometime after 11 p.m., Jen O'Malley Dillon called and spoke with Ruiz. All eyes were on Pennsylvania. The vice president was trailing in the state, but there were still enough votes out that she could come back and win, O'Malley Dillon told her. North Carolina was still reachable, and Georgia was doable still, and she felt optimistic about Arizona and Nevada. Biden called a friend, former Pennsylvania congressman Bob Brady, to see what he knew. Then the president called Governor Josh Shapiro and they spoke for several minutes. After hanging up, the president addressed the room. "He said she's behind and she'd have to win what's left with a percentage that they don't think is going to be there," Biden said. "So what he said was 'Look, it's still possible, but I'm not seeing anything that suggests that it's going to happen.'" Biden paused. Then he said, "It looks like Trump is going to win."

AT THE NAVAL OBSERVATORY, THE VICE PRESIDENT AND HER team were batting out a statement for Harris to deliver at Howard. Hundreds of young people were packed into the courtyard there watching the returns on a large television screen. It was supposed to be a joyous night—a celebration of the first Black, female president-elect of the United States. It was about to be something else entirely. "We were working on the statement," said an adviser. "And then it just started to feel like things were shifting so that it wouldn't make sense to go out and say, 'We have all these positive signs of a victory.' It was a little uncertain there around 11:30 p.m. to midnight. It started to sound like maybe Pennsylvania was going to get called. And that Trump might go out and do a speech."

There was troubling news from Georgia. At 12:35 a.m., CNN projected that Trump would win there, carrying his second battleground state (after North Carolina)—and confirming O'Malley Dillon's earlier assessment that the sunbelt states were lost. "We didn't like what we were seeing out of Georgia," said an adviser. "So that's when, I can't remember who called whom. We were like, 'What the fuck's going on?'"

Voles had summoned a photographer and a videographer; they were supposed to head to Howard with the vice president for a victory speech.

The moment of truth came just after midnight. O'Malley Dillon huddled with her two best analytics experts. They were O'Malley's barometer, her north star--and when they told her they didn't see a path to victory, O'Malley Dillon knew there wasn't one. She called the vice president. "We're down in the Blue Wall states and we're not going to be able to make it up," she said. "Oh, my God," said Harris. "What is going to happen to this country?"

Suddenly it was over—as though someone had thrown a switch. "We sent people home," said an aide. "I'm not sure what time it was. We just said, 'Go home.' And then, 'Find Cedric.'" Cedric Richmond, a Harris confidant, was tapped to deliver the bad news to the faithful at Howard. He took the stage at 12:45 a.m. There would be no declaration of victory that night. There would be no Harris presidency.

At about 1 a.m., Jen O'Malley Dillon faced one of her most daunting tasks. She had to call her twelve-year-old, twin daughters. They'd been knocking on doors for Harris in Arizona that weekend and were totally invested in the campaign. They'd sent their mother a note saying they had to go to bed but that they knew the numbers were going to turn for Harris. O'Malley Dillon called them on Facetime to give them the news. And that was the moment when Jen O'Malley Dillon, the steely, take-no-prisoners campaign manager, broke down.

As her devastated followers departed, the ground was littered with discarded American flags and a Harris-Walz poster.

It was 2:30 a.m. when Donald Trump took the stage at the Palm Beach County Convention Center. He was greeted by cries of "U.S.A."—the same chant that had echoed three months earlier at the DNC in Chicago. "This was, I believe, the greatest political movement of all time, there's never been anything like it in this country—and maybe beyond," Trump declared. J.D. Vance, the vice president–elect, made brief remarks. Then Trump called out to the woman who, more than anyone else, had resurrected his political career against all odds. "Susie, come up here," he said. "The Ice Maiden, we call her the Ice Maiden." Susie Wiles shyly stepped forward and then quickly retreated. "Susie likes to stay in the background, she's not in the background," Trump said.

Indeed, Wiles would soon become Trump's incoming White House chief of staff, the first woman to hold the second most powerful job in government.

Later that morning, the day after the election, Sheila Nix went over to the Naval Observatory. She met Voles in the back office. There was no time to wallow; among the first orders of business was arranging the vice president's call to concede the election to Trump. Nix called the president-elect on her cell phone—but for some reason couldn't merge the call with the vice president's phone. So Voles called Harris on hers—and she and Nix pressed their phones together. Voles held out both hands together to demonstrate. "The vice president is on the line," she said.

Harris respectfully addressed the man she'd called a fascist and an existential threat to democracy. After 107 days of adrenaline-fueled campaigning, she felt the weight of a crushing defeat. But unlike Trump four years earlier, she was respecting the election result. "I'm calling to concede," Harris said. "It was a fair election. The peaceful transfer of power is important. It's important to the country." And then she added, pointedly, "I hope you're a president for all Americans."

If Trump detected any edge to that remark, he didn't show it. In fact, the president-elect was weirdly cordial and complimentary—bantering as though he were on the golf course. "You were great," he said. "You're a tough cookie. You were really great. And that Doug—what a character! I love that guy." One of Harris's aides found this odd and inappropriate. "I was like, what?" she recalled. "Honestly, I felt like, what is this? It's so manipulative. He's a sociopath. But the phone call was fine. And she was lovely. I mean, she was appropriate."

At Harvard's John F. Kennedy School a few weeks later, Sheila Nix would say that Harris had run "a nearly flawless campaign." Indeed, in the weeks after Biden dropped off the ticket, Harris had seized the nomination, mobilized a formidable presidential campaign apparatus almost overnight, raked in record amounts of money, raised her approval rating by an astonishing 16 points, and outpointed Trump in their only debate. Even a perfect campaign might have faltered against the worldwide tide of anger and economic discontent that had swept incumbents away since COVID struck in 2020. (During that period, 40 out of 54 incumbent parties were defeated at the ballot box in western democracies.) But Harris's campaign was far from flawless.

It will take time, and access to more data than I have at this writing, to discern all the factors that contributed to her defeat.

Harris's failure to answer the "They/Them" attack ad was surely one of them. More telling was her inability to persuade enough Americans that she represented change.

In the end, Jennifer O'Malley Dillon's formidable ground game was vanquished by a ragtag band of amateurs throwing Hail Mary passes. But it was actually Pat Summerall's daughter, Susie Wiles, who'd coached the team to victory—grinding out yardage one down at a time. Three yards and a cloud of dust.

Manafort was dismissive of O'Malley Dillon's vaunted campaign machine. "We had a better organization than they did," he said. "We didn't need the same number of people. We had a very laser-focused approach and we had an organization that served that approach. And we turned out the vote where we needed to turn it out." He continued: "They couldn't turn out the tough vote. They couldn't turn out the early vote. So what did they accomplish? They turned out the base that was going to vote anyhow."

Manafort also argued that Trump neutralized the two issues Harris focused on at the end. "With the 'save democracy people,' we split that. We were fifty-fifty on people who voted on that issue. On abortion, we narrowed that difference to almost nothing."

Manafort went on: "The story of how she lost was as much about who didn't turn out to vote for her as who turned out to vote for us. There was a reason we hammered, for $40 million worth, the transgender ad. It wasn't because of the issue of transgender. It was the issue that there's ninety-five percent of the country that's normal and there's five percent of the country, meaning Harris and company, who think that should be normal. Very few people believed prisoners should have federally funded sex-change operations. And we had her saying that at the camera. It isolated her as an extremist and outside the norm. And then you isolate her with fracking and with Medicare [during her 2019 campaign, Harris had opposed fracking and supported Medicare for all] and eventually even moderates and liberals say she's too tough to swallow. And 'I can't vote for Trump, but I'm just not going to vote,' and they didn't vote."

One of her top advisers insisted that Harris had done everything she could. "I think she really did get to the point where she was able to talk about how she would be a different kind of leader, a new generation, and what that means and what she would focus on going forward. I think she was able to make the distinction between her and Biden on how they would govern."

But the truth was she didn't. Harris and her team were too attached to the Biden-Harris record to do what needed to be done.

"Joe Biden and Kamala Harris managed the post-pandemic recovery better than almost any country," said one of her top advisers. "And if you compare the data from the other countries, we did much, much better. We avoided a recession. We kept job growth. Inflation was lower than other countries."

All of that was true. But none of it mattered to Americans fed up with the cost of putting bread on the table—and the sense that Harris cared more about "They/them" than about working-class Americans.

FIVE WEEKS AFTER THE ELECTION, I VISITED LORRAINE VOLES IN her office on the second floor of the Eisenhower Executive Office Building, across the West Wing parking lot from the White House. Next to the reception area is the vice president's ornate ceremonial office, decorated with framed paintings of admirals and ship models. Harris has used it to sign special declarations and as a quiet retreat from the political fray. A big mahogany desk—which once sat in the Oval Office—is the first thing you see. And inside the top drawer, every vice president since Nelson Rockefeller had carved his name. Soon Harris would be carving hers there, too. According to her chief of staff, the outgoing vice president has no firm plans for the future.

After the election, a senior Harris aide's husband told her, "You keep talking about democracy and I keep talking about six-dollar eggs.'" He wasn't the only one. A few days earlier, one of Voles's colleagues on the campaign had shared a story with me.

That morning, something had happened that crystallized the election's outcome in a way that all the pollsters and data experts never could. She was speaking on the phone to her daughter, just a few years out of college. A political junkie like her mother, she'd taken a friend to a doctor's appointment. Afterward, they decided to get a snack. "They never go to McDonald's," said her mother, "but there was one across the street. So they went to McDonald's and whatever they got cost twenty-six dollars. And she was like, 'Oh my God, twenty-six dollars! That's so much!' And it's the first time she personally felt, 'Oh my God, this used to cost twelve!' She's like, 'Now I'm starting to understand: You can't talk people out of that feeling.'"

It was the lesson of the 2024 presidential campaign, the wildest and perhaps most consequential in U.S. history.

"IT DIDN'T SEEM LIKE SHE EVEN TRIED"

O n November 6, the morning after the 2024 election, the second-guessing, finger-pointing, and backstabbing began: How had a convicted felon who'd inspired an attempted insurrection, bungled a once-in-a-century pandemic, and left office in disgrace pulled off the biggest political comeback in history? And how had an eminently qualified nominee, a Black and Asian woman who'd unified her party, raised more than $1 billion, and inspired a new generation, lost the most consequential election of modern times?

As the bitter postmortem began, the candidates and their principal deputies were scattering across the country.

Kamala Harris and Doug Emhoff flew to Hawaii for a week-long stay in a rented villa. Jen O'Malley Dillon spent Thanksgiving with her extended family in Massachusetts. Donald Trump held court at Mar-a-Lago, picking cabinet nominees with his son Donald Jr. and constant companion Elon Musk; one of Trump's first postelection decisions was to appoint Susie Wiles as his incoming White House chief of staff. Jared Kushner and Ivanka

Trump reaffirmed their decision to stay out of politics; while he spoke almost daily with Trump's Middle East envoy Steve Witkoff, Jared would not be returning to the White House. Chris LaCivita and Corey Lewandowski weren't going there, either, but they weren't leaving quietly; on election night, they'd hurled f-bombs at each other before leaving the Palm Beach Convention Center.

For Paul Manafort, Trump's victory represented a potential windfall, a resurrection of his career as a lucrative international lobbyist. On January 12 *The New York Times* reported that Manafort, along with others from Trump's 2024 campaign, had been pitching his services to far-right political factions in Latin America and Europe—including Ukraine, where his shady entanglements had gotten him fired from Trump's 2016 campaign. When we spoke the day before Trump's 2025 inauguration, Manafort confirmed that he was talking to overseas political parties about doing business with them. He shrugged off the *New York Times* report. "It's what I've been doing for the last thirty-five years," he said. "It's just now I'm bringing along the guys who ran the last winning presidential election."

It was time to ask him about the mysterious case of that Ferdinand Marcos crony and the missing suitcase allegedly stuffed with $10 million in cash (a story I told in chapter 1). According to Ed Rollins, Ronald Reagan's 1984 campaign manager, an associate of the late Philippines dictator told him that Manafort had absconded with an illegal $10 million–dollar contribution from Marcos to Reagan's campaign.

"Just one more thing," I said to Manafort. "Ed Rollins wrote in his memoir that on a trip to Manila, a Marcos crony told him, 'I was the guy who gave the $10 million from Marcos to your campaign.' And Rollins replied, 'Who did you give the cash to?'

Rollins said the crony named a very well-known Washington power lobbyist who was involved in the campaign. Was it you?"

Manafort shook his head. "I don't think it's true, by the way," he said. "I don't think it's true. The story. I don't think the story is true."

I pressed him. "In his memoir Rollins said it was a very well-known Washington lobbyist. Now he says on the record that it was you. What do you say to that?"

Manafort waved his hand as if swatting at a mosquito. "Same thing," he said. The charge was just nonsense from an old political foe.

IN THE ELECTION'S AFTERMATH, ANIMOSITY BETWEEN THE TRUMP and Harris campaigns was palpable. In mid-January I spoke with Susie Wiles and Jen O'Malley Dillon in separate back-to-back interviews. In presidential campaigns, as in military operations, victory has a thousand fathers, and defeat is an orphan—because while Wiles spoke freely without conditions, O'Malley Dillon would only speak on background.

Democrats wanted to know why Harris had lost to Trump and his MAGA movement. Susie Wiles wanted to know why Harris and her team had run such a flawed campaign.

Wiles called me from her car on a Saturday morning as she was driving up I-95 from Mar-a-Lago to her home in Ponte Vedra Beach, Florida, a four-hour trip. She was in high spirits— and insisted she'd never doubted that Trump would win. "At no point did I think we would not win. Not internally, not in my core, not in my sleep, not in my rational mind," she said. "I never believed he would lose."

Indeed, what had sounded like arrogance on the part of

Trump's handlers just a few months earlier now appeared to be well-founded confidence. But Wiles didn't believe that Trump's victory was inevitable. Some observers, including Harris campaign staffers, were arguing that no Democratic nominee could have overcome the worldwide rejection of incumbent parties that had taken place since the pandemic struck in 2020. I asked Wiles: Did that mean Harris couldn't have won? Trump's campaign chair didn't mince words. "We'll never know," she replied, "because it didn't seem like she even tried."

That was an incendiary charge to lob at Harris, but Wiles was just warming up. On the campaign trail, she said, the vice president had come off as timid and phony. "She was so underexposed and controlled, and people like realism," Wiles said. "Voters want authenticity. And they didn't get that from her." It was true that, coming out of an electrifying convention, Harris had seemed flat-footed; she was accused of ducking interviews with mainstream media. O'Malley Dillon insisted that Harris wasn't ducking anything—and blamed the press for failing to hold Trump to the same standard. But Trump was known and Harris was not. Her failure to quickly define herself gave Trump the opening to paint her as a woke leftist radical. "She's in a mixed-race marriage with a California liberal, a prosecutor with a very odd record, trying to assume the mantle of something [the Biden record] that wasn't popular," said Wiles. "I mean, that's tough. Maybe no tougher than being eighty-seven times indicted or whatever. But it's a tough cocktail."

O'Malley Dillon countered that Harris had come out of Chicago with a compelling, nuanced message—on what she called the opportunity economy, affordable housing, the sandwich generation (people caring for children and aging parents), and lower costs. She'd gone to the southern border and rolled out a new immigration policy. And as O'Malley Dillon saw it, Harris had made a strong case for why Trump would be worse than ever.

Wiles and O'Malley Dillon weren't strangers. They'd met at a political event—and Harris's campaign chair had phoned her GOP counterpart after Trump's close brush with a would-be assassin in Pennsylvania. They'd spoken several times during the campaign. "Jen O'Malley is a little bit of a friend," Wiles told me. "When we get to Washington, I'm going to go see her." It was hard to tell if Wiles was being serious—or trolling her defeated rival.

"What do you want to ask her?" I said. Wiles replied, "I want to ask her why they kept Harris in the 2024 version of the basement."

Wiles was referring to Biden's phoning in of his 2020 campaign—for which COVID had given him an excuse—and argued that Harris's handlers were hiding *her* because she wasn't up to the task. Of Harris's performance on the campaign trail, Wiles said, "We couldn't believe how bad she was." Harris's failure to distance herself from Biden on *The View,* she said, was exactly what her campaign staff must have feared: "The only thing I can conclude is they didn't think she could deliver."

When I relayed this to Jen O'Malley Dillon, I could practically hear her jaw clench. Who was standing on the debate stage destroying Donald Trump at every turn? she asked. After their single debate, Trump never stood on a stage with her again. Why, O'Malley Dillon wondered, was he was so afraid of that? And, Harris's campaign chair insisted, the more people saw the candidate, the more they liked her.

What about the candidates' running mates? Wiles was blunt: "Tim Walz represented everything that we were running against." He was "the poster child of somebody lying about their service to the country. His abortion record was far to the left of the mainstream of the country." According to Wiles, Harris's choice of the avuncular Minnesota governor over the sharp-tongued Josh Shapiro, the governor of Pennsylvania, helped seal Harris's fate. "Pretty quickly," Wiles said, "the luster seemed to come off her." (Choosing Shapiro wouldn't have changed the election outcome, Wiles argued, but it would have forced Trump to spend more time and money in Pennsylvania.)

O'Malley Dillon replied with a spirited defense of Walz. J.D. Vance's rollout, she pointed out, with his remarks about childless cat ladies, had been a fiasco. In a general election, she added, no one votes for a vice-presidential candidate. O'Malley Dillon knew that, and so did Wiles.

In the end, no matter how much they argued their cases after the fact, the result was the same. In an election that was supposed to be whisker-close, Trump carried every battleground state. Still, a victory margin of 1.5 percent in the popular vote was no landslide or basis for a mandate. Nor was Trump's victory a foregone conclusion. One former Democratic presidential campaign manager was blunt: "We've all decided Harris was never going to win it. That's bullshit."

Researching this book, I spoke to scores of political observers, operatives, and analysts from both sides of the aisle. But as Trump's inauguration approached, I wanted to hear from one person who, when it comes to politics and governance, cuts to the heart of the matter.

Leon Edward Panetta, eighty-six, the former OMB director, congressman, White House chief of staff, CIA director, and secretary of defense, has seen a few campaigns over his five-decade career. He saw the 2024 race unfold from his walnut farm near Carmel, California. That was where he had watched Joe Biden self-destruct against Donald Trump during the June 27 debate. Panetta had been on the phone with his former CIA chief of staff Jeremy Bash. It was still fresh in Panetta's mind when we spoke in mid-January.

"We both had the same reaction: This is our worst nightmare," Panetta recalled. "This confirms every suspicion that people had about Joe Biden's ability. And for that to happen, and for him to even then hold on—I just think it made it that much tougher for Kamala Harris to establish her own identity."

Panetta believed that Harris's campaign had failed its most important test. "The failing was not to sit in a room and say, 'What is your vision? What is your identity that you want to convey to the American people as to who you are?' She had to appear as her own person to establish her identity and to move on." But in Panetta's view, Harris didn't accomplish that.

Moving on meant clearly separating herself from Joe Biden. "That's the name of the game," Panetta said. "You've got to be willing to do that. And they were just too hesitant. I thought they were thinking they could tiptoe into the presidency without getting anybody pissed off at them. Baloney. You've got to make the American people understand that you're tough enough to be president of the United States."

Panetta had been Joe Biden's friend for fifty years. "One of the great failings of Joe Biden is his failure to prevent Donald Trump from getting reelected," he said. "Biden could not have won if he had stayed in." Panetta faulted the president for "his inability to see that at an early stage, where it could have made a difference in the competition that would have taken place in order to get the nomination."

History, Panetta believed, would come down hard on the men and women around the forty-sixth president. "I think they've been living in an isolated world," he said. "The White House is an isolating place. The challenge is to break out of that and try to stay in touch with the rest of the world as much as you can. And I don't think that happened here."

On the eve of Trump's inauguration, Biden's true believers were still in a state of denial. When I spoke to Biden's longtime aide Mike Donilon in late January, he still believed that the party had made a terrible mistake in running away from a well-known incumbent president with a consequential record.

Even O'Malley Dillon, against overwhelming evidence, thought Biden could have won. Her judgment was clouded by her single-minded focus on the metrics of the race. After the president's disastrous debate, O'Malley Dillon's first thought wasn't "How can we talk to the president about stepping aside?" It was that not that many people had actually seen the debate. This betrayed a lack of political acumen—and common sense. O'Malley Dillon believed her dial groups more than her lying eyes.

Panetta observed, "Everybody was marching to the same tune. And there was nobody there to say, 'What the hell's going on?' They just never had a grown-up in the room who could look Joe Biden in the eye and say, 'What the fuck are you doing?'"

And yet the truth was that an earlier decision by Biden to step aside might not have changed the outcome of the 2024 presidential race. A longer primary might have given the eventual Democratic nominee—Harris or someone else—more opportunities to make mistakes. Moreover, Democratic primaries tend to push candidates to their left ideologically—which was where Harris went in her ill-fated 2019 bid. It's entirely possible that a Democratic nominee, battered and bloodied by an extended primary fight, might have limped into the general election in a weakened state.

But that unpredictable possibility was no argument for Biden to stay in the race—or for avoiding the rigors of a Democratic primary process. "If we're afraid of that," said Panetta, "then we'll fail as a party. If we just give up and say, 'Oh no, we just can't take on the left,' then we'll fail. Bill Clinton appeased the left and at the same time established his own credentials as to who he was. And Joe Biden got the shit kicked out of him in New Hampshire and Iowa—but he came back in South Carolina."

The Democratic party had the deepest reservoir of talent in generations, but no one except Dean Phillips stepped up to challenge Biden for the nomination. "In a democracy, we govern either by leadership or by crisis," said Panetta. "And leadership requires the ability to make tough decisions, to take risks, and to sometimes offend those that are closest to you. If we don't have that kind of leadership, then we'll govern by crisis. And I think that if you look at the period that you're writing about, it is a reflection of failed leadership on all levels, not only on the Democratic side but on the Republican side as well."

Ultimately, reckoning with the 2024 presidential campaign requires coming to grips with the powerful popular appeal of an angry demagogue with no record of delivering the results he promises. And that requires a clear-eyed look at middle-class Americans' decades-old belief that Democratic party elites have betrayed them. "This is without question the Trump era," said Panetta. "And it's the Trump era for reasons that are very real out there in the country. And we've got to spend some time really trying to understand the chemistry that produced this era. And where was the leadership that failed to deal with what was happening in the country? Because we now bear the fruit of that failed leadership."

Failed leadership produced a president who promised not

only to lower high prices and fix the southern border but to pursue retribution, pardon January 6 insurrectionists—which he did on his first day—and prosecute his political enemies without evidence. Hours before Trump took the oath of office for a second term, Joe Biden felt compelled to grant preemptive pardons to Anthony Fauci, General Mark Milley, members of the January 6 committee, and the U.S. Capitol and D.C. Metropolitan Police officers who testified before the select committee. They were men and women who had simply done their jobs. Biden also pardoned five members of his family.

During his first term as president, Trump governed the same way he'd campaigned: demonizing opponents and making seat-of-the-pants decisions without anyone who could put a brake on his worst instincts. In his second term, he has an advantage that eluded him the first time around: a White House chief of staff, Susie Wiles, who has shown an uncanny ability to impose discipline on his disorder.

The woman who helped Trump beat Biden, Harris, and the odds in the wildest campaign in history now carries a profound responsibility. She represents the thin line between the president and disaster.

Chris Whipple
January 21, 2025
Clinton, Connecticut

ACKNOWLEDGMENTS

This book couldn't have been written without Lisa Sharkey, the force of nature and senior VP of HarperCollins. Last summer, I was immersed in reporting and writing a book about presidential campaign managers, *The Kingmakers*—which Lisa had commissioned—when the political world suddenly turned upside down. Joe Biden's abdication and Kamala Harris's ascension as the Democratic nominee against Donald Trump was the political campaign story of the century. It was a book of its own and it needed to be written quickly. I suggested to Lisa that I put *The Kingmakers* aside, temporarily, and write the story of Biden, Harris, Trump, and the wildest election campaign in U.S. history. Lisa readily agreed to the idea—and threw her team behind it. The result is *Uncharted*.

Writing a book on the 2024 presidential campaign while it was still unfolding was like designing Apollo 13 while it was hurtling to Earth. While I had an extraordinary team supporting me every step of the way, landing it sometimes felt like undergoing reentry without a heat shield—the whole thing could have been blown to smithereens at any moment.

I couldn't have done it without Lisa's excellent, cool-headed team: my talented editor, Maddie Pillari, editorial assistant Lexie Von Zedlitz, publicity director Kate D'Esmond, marketing man-

ACKNOWLEDGMENTS

ager Sam Lubash, production manager Diana Meunier, production editor Lydia Weaver, and interior designer Nancy Singer. Milan Bozic not only created a spectacular cover, he had to design two versions—one with Trump and the other with Harris at the forefront, looking victorious, depending on the election result. And of course he ended up with Trump. Mike Bzozowski, HarperCollins's lawyer, made the legal vetting process a pleasure, and I'm sure saved me from myself.

David Hume Kennerly, my friend and partner on political documentaries, and the Center for Creative Photography at the University of Arizona, which houses his archive, generously contributed many of the superb photos in this book. He also read chapters in progress and gave me great notes. Other early readers who offered valuable suggestions were Mark McKinnon, political campaign strategist *extraordinaire*; Leon Panetta, Bill Clinton's superb White House chief; Greg Zorthian, former president of the *Financial Times* in America; and Lisa Queen, my good friend and amazing literary agent. Jack Watson, my dear friend and Jimmy Carter's White House chief of staff, not only read early chapters but provided his usual, eagle-eyed copyediting.

The majority of interviews for this book were conducted on "deep background," meaning that I promised not to attribute what I learned to anyone without permission. So most of my sources will remain anonymous. They know who they are and I'm enormously grateful to them.

But others won't mind if I thank them in these pages. To put the 2024 presidential race into context, I was fortunate to tap into an extraordinary network of former campaign managers and advisers. They are a rogues' gallery (though many are women) of political junkies, nerds, and geniuses who not only taught me about the ins and outs of running these multibillion-dollar enterprises; they provided rich historical background for understanding the 2024 campaign.

They are (chronologically, by presidential candidate): Gary Hart and Rick Ridder (George McGovern); Dwight Chapin (Richard Nixon); Gerald Rafshoon (Jimmy Carter); Stu Spencer, Ed Rollins, and Rich Bond (Ronald Reagan); Mary Matalin (George H.W. Bush); Billy Shore and John Emerson (Gary Hart); James Carville, George Stephanopoulos, and Mandy Grunwald (Bill Clinton); Robert Shrum (Al Gore); Karl Rove and Mark McKinnon (George W. Bush); Stuart Stevens (John McCain); Jim Messina and Jennifer Ridder (Barack Obama); and Tim Miller (Jeb Bush).

I wanted to understand what made Biden, Harris, Trump—and their advisers—tick. As Richard Ben Cramer put it in his classic work, *What It Takes*: "I wanted to know enough about these people to *see* . . . once they decided to run, and marched (or slid or flung themselves headlong) into this semi-rational, all-consuming quest . . . what happened to those lives . . . what did *we do to them*, on the way to the White House?"

To find out, I had to get inside the Biden, Harris, and Trump campaigns—in mid-flight.

Talk about *Uncharted:* Navigating Trump World requires a guide who knows the dangerous terrain, and few know it better than Paul Manafort. I'm grateful to him for guiding me through Trump palace intrigues from Mar-a-Lago to Bedminster to the campaign trail. During frequent Zoom sessions, he kept me apprised of Trump's 2024 campaign strategy and trusted me not to share it with anyone before publication. I also drew on a long acquaintance with Jared and Ivanka Kushner, who graciously invited me to their house for long conversations on multiple occasions during Trump's first term as president. Kellyanne Conway,

ACKNOWLEDGMENTS

Corey Lewandowski, and Brad Parscale also sat for insightful interviews.

Biden World is in many ways more difficult to penetrate than the Trump jungle. From the start, the Biden White House assumed a defensive crouch toward journalists. But I was fortunate to strike up productive, long-running conversations with two excellent White House chiefs of staff: Ron Klain and Jeffrey Zients. Saloni Sharma, senior adviser for communications to Zients, was a delight to work with. And I was fortunate to sit down for interviews with almost all of Biden's close advisers, including Steve Ricchetti, Bruce Reed, Bob Bauer, and Ted Kaufman.

For my reporting on Joe Biden's campaign and his decision to step aside, I depended on Greg Schultz, Ben LaBolt, and Michael LaRosa. To understand Kamala Harris's historic, whirlwind campaign, I relied on her chiefs of staff Lorraine Voles and Sheila Nix; senior adviser Brian Fallon; and Jennifer Palmieri, who ran second gentleman Douglas Emhoff's campaign.

As always, I'm grateful for the insights provided by former White House chiefs of staff, many of whom have become my friends: Leon Panetta, James A. Baker III, Ron Klain, Jeff Zients, Bill Daley, Thomas H. "Mack" McLarty, Erskine Bowles, Reince Priebus, and Jack Watson.

I'm grateful to other experts who helped me understand the campaign: historians Mark Updegrove and Doug Brinkley; Senator Richard Blumenthal, Democrat of Connecticut; Peter Baker; Arnon Mishkin; Leslie Dach; John Gizzi; Norm Eisen; and my *Vanity Fair* colleague Molly Jong-Fast.

A salute to good friends who helped keep me going: Josh and Alex Getlin and Heidi Evans; Nancy Collins; David and Liz Chidekel; Trip McCrossin; Donna Parsons; Lee Westerberg;

ACKNOWLEDGMENTS

Jim Caulkins and Evelyne Vaquero; Susan Zirinsky and Joe Peyronnin; Jules and Jacqueline Naudet; Gedeon Naudet and Aude Coquatrix; Ward and Susan Pennebaker; Jon Meyersohn and Julie Hartenstein; Angela Chambers; Bruce McIntosh; Paul Trachtman; David Friend and Nancy Paulsen; Judy Twersky; Milt Kass; John and Anda Hutchins; KC and Ann Ramsay; Jeff and Annie VanNest; Brian Ross; Ray Lambiase; Paige Peterson; Patricia Duff and Richard Cohen; Harry and Gigi Benson; Don Dahler; David Glinert; Vicki Harmer and Jed Becker; April Peveteaux; Esme, Judah, and Aaron Goldman; Norma Burke; Peter and Ann Ross; Anush and Sholeh Djhabani; Charles Tremayne and Caroline Grist; Sharon Lerner; and Cynthia McFadden.

Finally, my family made it all possible. My nieces, Abby and Melissa, and their spouses, David and Gary, and all of the Dofts—Jamie, Matthew, Lucy, and Tory—put up with my unending campaign stories. My sister Ann Marr provided her usual brilliant copyediting, editorial advice, love, and encouragement. Sam Whipple, to whom this book is dedicated, will be running his own campaign someday. And my wife, Cary, who never signed up for this, is the best partner—in book writing and in life—that I can imagine.

ENDNOTES

INTRODUCTION

1 "He didn't know what Trump had been saying": Ron Klain, interview with author, September 8, 2024.

2 "I must be a great president": Ibid.

2 "Ragin' Cajun": Jonathan Martin, "Mapping the Carville Era, from Bill Clinton's Alter Ego to Joe Biden's Bete Noire," *Politico*, October 5, 2024, https://www.politico.com/news/magazine/2024/10/05/mapping-the-carville -era-from-bill-clintons-alter-ego-to-joe-bidens-bete-noire-00182589.

3 "'He needs to get out": Ron Klain, interview with author, September 8, 2024.

6 "He didn't really understand what his argument was": Ibid.

6 "people just think you're perplexed": Ibid.

6 "There was no reason to be early": Ibid.

7 "This is a disaster": Ibid.

7 "You did such a great job": Alan Blinder, "At One Post-Debate Party, President Biden Found a Jubilant Reception," *New York Times*, June 28, 2024, https://www.nytimes.com/2024/06/28/us/biden-debate-watch-party.html.

9 "bad night": Toluse Olorunnipa, Tyler Pager, and Michael Scherer, "Biden Team Works Furiously to Quell Any Democratic Revolt After Debate," *Washington Post*, June 30, 2024, https://www.washingtonpost.com/poli tics/2024/06/30/biden-democrats-election/.

10 *The Godfather*: Eli Stokols, Lauren Egan, and Ben Johansen, "Leave the Dunn. Take the Cannoli," *Politico*, August 20, 2024, https://www.polit ico.com/newsletters/west-wing-playbook/2024/08/20/leave-the-dunn -take-the-cannolis-00175121.

11 "bloody battle": Ron Klain, interview with author, September 8, 2024.

CHAPTER 1: "I SAW THE DAGGERS COMING OUT OF HIS EYES."

13 "It only got worse from there": Paul Manafort, interview with author, March 19, 2024.

14 "you're a good-looking guy": Corey R. Lewandowski and David N. Bossie, *Let Trump Be Trump* (New York: Center Street, 2017).

14 "to secure his youthful appearance": Ibid.

14 "Manafort was a leaker": Ibid.

14 $100,000: Andrew Weissmann, *Where Law Ends: Inside the Mueller Investigation* (New York: Random House, 2020).

15 "the natural": Joe Klein, *The Natural: The Misunderstood Presidency of Bill Clinton* (New York: Crown, 2003).

15 "this is Donald Trump": Kellyanne Conway, interview with author, September 18, 2024.

15 "stealing my victories": Paul Manafort, interview with author, March 19, 2024.

15 the famous "postmortem": Garance Franke-Ruta, "What You Need to Read in the RNC Election-Autopsy Report," *Atlantic*, March 18, 2013, https://www.theatlantic.com/politics/archive/2013/03/what-you-need-to -read-in-the-rnc-election-autopsy-report/274112/.

16 "you don't know the rules": Paul Manafort, interview with author, March 19, 2024.

16 "Did you know any of this?": Ibid.

17 "from zero to frontrunner": Ibid.

17 "How do we use to get whole?": Julia Ioffe and Franklin Foer, "Did Manafort Use Trump to Curry Favor with a Putin Ally?," *Atlantic*, October 2, 2017, https://www.theatlantic.com/politics/archive/2017/10/emails -suggest-manafort-sought-approval-from-putin-ally-deripaska/541677/.

17 "it's all Corey's fault": Lewandowski and Bossie, *Let Trump Be Trump*.

18 "Am I a baby, Paul?": Ibid.

18 "Am I paying for these people?": Kellyanne Conway, email to author, December 23, 2024.

19 "vote your conscience": Patrick Healy and Jonathan Martin, "Ted Cruz Stirs Convention Fury in Pointed Snub of Donald Trump," *New York Times*, July 20, 2016, https://www.nytimes.com/2016/07/21/us/politics/ted -cruz-donald-trump-mike-pence-rnc.html.

19 "a highly successful convention": Jared Kushner, *Breaking History: A White House Memoir* (Detroit: Broadside, 2022).

19 Kathy: Michael Wolff, *Siege: Trump Under Fire* (Henry Holt and Co., 2019).

20 "Twelve-point-seven-million-dollar payment": Lewandowski and Bossie, *Let Trump Be Trump*.

20 "loot Ukrainian assets and influence elections": Andrew E. Kramer, Mike McIntire, and Barry Meier, "Secret Ledger in Ukraine Lists Cash for Donald Trump's Campaign Chief," *New York Times*, August 15, 2016, https:// www.nytimes.com/2016/08/15/us/politics/what-is-the-black-ledger.html.

21 "You can do anything": "Transcript: Donald Trump's Taped Comments About Women," *New York Times*, October 8, 2016, https://www.nytimes .com/2016/10/08/us/donald-trump-tape-transcript.html.

23 "kindly withdraw": Aaron C. Davis and Carol D. Leonnig, "$10M Cash Withdrawal Drove Secret Probe into Whether Trump Took Money from

Egypt," *Washington Post*, August 2, 2024, https://www.washingtonpost
.com/investigations/2024/08/02/trump-campaign-egypt-investigation/.

23 "people power revolution": Seth Mydans, "Throng in Manila Marks Day 'People Power' Triumphed," *New York Times*, May 26, 1986, https:// www.nytimes.com/1986/05/26/world/throng-in-manila-marks-day-peo ple-power-triumphed.html.

23 "You ran Reagan's campaign": Ed Rollins, *Bare Knuckles and Back Rooms: My Life in American Politics* (New York: Broadway, 1996).

25 "he would have walked across the stage and hit somebody": Greg Schultz, interview with author, May 23, 2024.

25 "Promise me, Dad": Joe Biden, *Promise Me, Dad: A Year of Hope, Hardship and Purpose* (New York: Flatiron, 2017).

25 "We just kept running": Greg Schultz, interview with author, May 23, 2024.

26 "out of time": *Washington Post* Staff, "Full Text: Biden's Announcement That He Won't Run for President," *Washington Post*, October 21, 2015, https://www.washingtonpost.com/news/post-politics/wp/2015/10/21 /full-text-bidens-announcement-that-he-wont-run-for-president/.

26 "I'll give you the money": Reuters, "Obama Offered to Help Biden Financially During Son's Illness," *Reuters*, January 12, 2021, https://www.reu ters.com/article/world/obama-offered-to-help-biden-financially-during -sons-illness-idUSKCN0UQ0O5/.

26 "the president was not encouraging": Biden, *Promise Me, Dad*.

27 "you've had a great career": Edward-Isaac Dovere, "When Obama Talked Biden Out of Running for President," *Atlantic*, April 25, 2019, https://www.theatlantic.com/politics/archive/2019/04/bidens-20202-an nouncement-brought-praise-obama/587989/.

28 "blue wall": Kinsey Crowley, "What Is the 'Blue Wall'? Latest Polls from Key States of Michigan, Pennsylvania, Wisconsin," *USA Today*, October 29, 2024, https://www.usatoday.com/story/news/politics/elec tions/2024/10/29/blue-wall-states/75912615007/.

28 "I regret it every day": Julia Zorthian, "Biden Says He Regrets Not Running for President 'Every Day,'" *Time*, January 7, 2016, https://time .com/4170922/joe-biden-regrets-not-running-president/.

28 "I can do it": Maggie Haberman, *Confidence Man: The Making of Donald Trump and the Breaking of America* (New York: Penguin, 2022).

CHAPTER 2: "WHY IS HE RUNNING?"

31 "the verb tenses changed:" Greg Schultz, interview by author, May 23, 2024.

32 "figuring out how to live": Hunter Biden, *Beautiful Things: A Memoir* (New York: Gallery Books, 2021).

33 "very fine people on both sides": Donald Trump, "Full Transcript and Video: Trump's News Conference in New York," *New York Times*, Au-

gust 15, 2017, https://www.nytimes.com/2017/08/15/us/politics/trump
-press-conference-transcript.html.

33 "Who are these guys?": Richard Ben Cramer, *What It Takes: The Way to the White House* (New York: Vintage, 1993).

33 "FDR Democrats": Greg Schultz, interview with author, May 23, 2024.

34 "Javanka" in the summer: David Smith, "Steve Bannon Savages 'Javanka', Laying Bare White House Tensions," *The Guardian*, December 23, 2017, https://www.theguardian.com/us-news/2017/dec/23/steve-bannon-savages
-javanka-laying-bare-white-house-tensions.

36 "acting chief" Mick Mulvaney: Michael Tackett and Maggie Haberman, "Trump Names Mick Mulvaney Acting Chief of Staff," *New York Times*, December 14, 2018, https://www.nytimes.com/2018/12/14/us/politics/mick
-mulvaney-trump-chief-of-staff.html.

37 "flipped" on Trump: Stephanie Mencimer, "Could Paul Manafort Still Flip on Donald Trump? An Ex-Justice Department Official Explains," *Mother Jones*, August 21, 2018, https://www.motherjones.com/politics/2018/08
/could-paul-manafort-still-flip-on-donald-trump/.

38 "Height is not depth": Kellyanne Conway, interview with the author, September 18, 2024.

39 "What the fuck?" he yelled: Michael C. Bender, *"Frankly, We Did Win This Election": The Inside Story of How Trump Lost* (New York: Twelve Books, 2021).

39 "Brad can make a million fucking dollars a month": Ibid.

39 vacation houses, boats, and a bright red: Jose Lambiet, "EXCLUSIVE: How Donald Trump's Campaign Manager Brad Parscale Went from Family Bankruptcy to Splashing Out Millions on Mansions, Condos and Luxury Cars Through His Companies That Get a Hefty Cut of the President's $57M Campaign Contributions," *Daily Mail*, August 22, 2019, https://www.dailymail.co.uk/news/article-7375719/Brad-Parscale
-fortune-companies-cut-Trumps-campaign-contributions.html.

39 "Meet Brad Parscale," announced: The Lincoln Project (@ProjectLincoln), "This is just another example that @realDonaldTrump is the worst manager America has ever seen. Don, you got conned . . . by your IT guy," Twitter (now X), May 20, 2020, https://x.com/ProjectLincoln/sta
tus/1263147585625305088.

42 "never seen a white man stand behind a Black man": Ibid.

42 "enemies list": Daniel Schorr, "Lives Well Lived: Richard Nixon, the Best of Enemies," *New York Times*, January 1, 1995, https://
www.nytimes.com/1995/01/01/magazine/lives-well-lived-richard
-nixon-the-best-of-enemies.html.

43 "we were within the margin of error in Oregon": Brad Parscale, interview with author, September 18, 2024.

44 "Trump Frustrated with Campaign Manager": Michael Scherer and Josh Dawsey, "Trump Frustrated with Campaign Manager Parscale Amid Falling Polls," *Washington Post*, July 12, 2020, https://www.washingtonpost

.com/politics/parscale-hits-a-rough-patch-as-trumps-campaign-manager/2020/07/12/4c53cd50-c1f8-11ea-b4f6-cb39cd8940fb_story.html.

45 "You're losing": Brad Parscale, interview with author, September 18, 2024.

45 "you're being demoted": Ibid.

45 "Can you believe this guy?": Kellyanne Conway, *Here's the Deal: A Memoir* (New York: Threshold Editions, 2022).

46 "hiding in his basement": Zeke Miller, "Trump Knocks Biden for Campaigning from Basement Amid Virus," Associated Press, May 8, 2020, https://apnews.com/article/d95718bfff3e5c7b07d58ab49bdb1e16.

46 "—his own campaign manager": Brad Parscale, interview with author, September 18, 2024.

47 "fraud on the American public": Donald Trump, Remarks from the East Room of the White House, November 4, 2020.

47 "the Big Steal": Ali Breland, "The Next 'Stop the Steal' Movement Is Here. The Right is already saying the election is rigged," *Atlantic*, October 28, 2024, https://www.theatlantic.com/technology/archive/2024/10/election-denial-stop-steal-trump-harris/680436/.

49 "Goodbye, we love you": Maggie Haberman, "Trump Departs Vowing, 'We Will Be Back in Some Form,'" *New York Times*, January 20, 2021, https://www.nytimes.com/2021/01/20/us/politics/trump-presidency.html.

CHAPTER 3: "EVERY FREAKING ONE OF THEM HAD NO BALLS."

50 "would not be the governor if not for Susie Wiles": Michael Kruse, "The Most Feared and Least Known Political Operative in America," *Politico Magazine*, April 26, 2024, https://www.politico.com/news/magazine/2024/04/26/susie-wiles-trump-desantis-profile-00149654.

50 "'let her go nicely'": Brad Parscale, interview with author, September 18, 2024.

50 "She won Florida": Michael C. Bender, *"Frankly, We Did Win This Election": The Inside Story of How Trump Lost* (New York: Twelve Books, 2021).

50 "She's calm": Kellyanne Conway, interview with author, September 18, 2024.

51 "my full-throated endorsement": Maggie Haberman, Donald Trump's Florida Effort Relied on Veteran of Gov. Rick Scott's Campaign," *New York Times*, March 15, 2016, https://archive.nytimes.com/www.nytimes.com/politics/first-draft/2016/03/15/donald-trumps-florida-effort-relied-on-veteran-of-gov-rick-scotts-campaign/.

51 "She is an expert": Kruse, "The Most Feared."

52 super PAC "Save America": Josh Dawsey and Isaac Stanley-Becker, "Susie Wiles Charted Trump's Comeback. Now She'll Manage His White House," *Washington Post*, November 8, 2024, https://www.washingtonpost.com/politics/2024/11/08/susie-wiles-trump-chief-staff/.

53 "Everything was scripted": Bill Daley, interview with author, August 12, 2024.

54 "virtually inconceivable": Ryan Lizza, "Biden Signals to Aides That He Would Serve Only a Single Term," *Politico*, December 11, 2019, https://www.politico.com/news/2019/12/11/biden-single-term-082129.

54 "I view myself as a bridge": Eric Bradner and Sarah Mucha, "Biden Says He's a 'Bridge' to New 'Generation of Leaders' While Campaigning with Harris, Booker, Whitmer," CNN, March 9, 2020, https://www.cnn.com/2020/03/09/politics/joe-biden-bridge-new-generation-of-leaders/index.html.

54 "we were having so much success getting things done": Joe Biden, *The View*, September 25, 2024.

54 "I don't remember any discussions": Ted Kaufman, interview with author, August 16, 2024.

55 "'How dare they?'": Kamala Harris, Remarks at the 2022 EMILY's List National Conference and Gala, Washington, D.C., May 3, 2022, https://www.whitehouse.gov/briefing-room/speeches-remarks/2022/05/03/remarks-by-vice-president-harris-at-the-2022-emilys-list-national-conference-and-gala/.

56 "You overturned Roe v. Wade": Meridith McGraw, *Trump in Exile* (New York: Random House, 2024).

56 "Swift Boat Veterans for Truth": Jodi Wilgoren, "Vietnam Veterans Buy Ads to Attack Kerry," *New York Times*, August 5, 2004, https://www.nytimes.com/2004/08/05/us/vietnam-veterans-buy-ads-to-attack-kerry.html.

57 "I'm very confident": Karl Rove, interview with author, January 18, 2024.

58 "America's most feared political operatives": Tim Alberta, "Trump Is Planning for a Landslide Win," *Atlantic*, July 10, 2024, https://www.theatlantic.com/politics/archive/2024/07/trump-campain-election-2024-susie-wiles-chris-lacivita/678806/.

58 "Inside the Terrifyingly Competent Trump 2024 Campaign": Gabriel Sherman, "Inside the Terrifyingly Competent Trump 2024 Campaign," *Vanity Fair*, April 4, 2024, https://www.vanityfair.com/news/inside-trump-2024-campaign?srsltid=AfmBOoo4WBBQnyxh4_2ATad5wNxXleqLtw6uLBDDnfy5JLIfB9DDBqu3.

58 "How worried should you be?": Ibid.

58 "having hunger and swagger": Kellyanne Conway, interview with author, September 18, 2024.

58 "few members of the 2016 team remain": Michael C. Bender, "Corey Lewandowski Was Fired in 2016. Why Is He Back at Trump's Side?," *New York Times*, September 17, 2024, https://www.nytimes.com/2024/09/17/us/politics/corey-lewandowski-trump-campaign.html.

58 "He does miss me": Kellyanne Conway, interview with author, September 18, 2024.

59 "red wave": Jim Rutenberg, Ken Bensinger, and Steve Eder, "The 'Red

Wave' Washout: How Skewed Polls Fed a False Election Narrative," *New York Times*, December 31, 2022, https://www.nytimes.com/2022/12/31/us /politics/polling-election-2022-red-wave.html.

60 "I love my father very much": Brooke Singman, "Ivanka Trump Says She Loves Her Father But Does 'Not Plan to Be Involved in Politics,'" *Fox News*, November 15, 2022, https://www.foxnews.com/politics/ivanka -trump-says-she-loves-her-father-does-not-plan-involved-politics.

61 video emphasizing "freedom": Andrea Shalal and Trevor Hunnicutt, "Biden Launches Campaign Video, Republicans Respond with Dysto-pian Vision," Reuters, April 25, 2023, https://www.reuters.com/world/us /bidens-campaign-video-stresses-personal-freedom-attacks-extremists-20 23-04-25/.

61 "There has to be one good Challenger X out there": Mark Leibovich, "The Case for a Primary Challenge to Joe Biden," *Atlantic*, February 27, 2023, https://www.theatlantic.com/politics/archive/2023/02/joe-biden-2024-elect ion-democrat-candidates/673212/?utm_campaign=the-atlantic&utm_con tent=edit-promo&utm_medium=social&utm_source=facebook&utm_term =2023-02-27T10%3A01%3A56&fbclid=IwY2xjawGvJdNleHRuA2Fl bQIxMQABHcKLEf0BwyNbj7zgzVe81mwLZtIh0lSmxd8vFDjGVWoqM lMRtJFght5IXQ_aem_z2HVH09fwc8at2CsXsjwVg.

62 "the internal polling only got worse": Bill Daley, interview with author, August 12, 2024.

62 "I think it would have just been hard": Jennifer Ridder, interview with author, August 29, 2024.

CHAPTER 4: "HOW ARE THEY LETTING THIS THING GO ON?"

65 "we have rewritten the political map!": Brett Samuels, "DeSantis Touts Florida's 'Rewritten' Political Map as Supporters Chant 'Two More Years,'" *The Hill*, November 8, 2022, https://thehill.com/homenews /campaign/3726275-desantis-touts-floridas-rewritten-political-map-as-su pporters-chant-two-more-years/.

65 "designed less for a reelection party": Matt Dixon and Gary Fineout, "De-Santis Wins Big, with an Eye Toward 2024," *Politico*, November 8, 2022, https://www.politico.com/news/2022/11/08/florida-governor-2022-ron -desantis-charlie-crist-00065788.

66 "DeFUTURE": Cover, *New York Post*, November 9, 2022, https://nypost .com/cover/november-9-2022/.

66 "Wow! The DeSantus": Julia Shapero, "Trump Blasts DeSantis Cam-paign Launch: 'Catastrophe,' 'DISASTER,'" *The Hill*, May 24, 2023, https://thehill.com/homenews/campaign/4019994-trump-blasts-desantis -campaign-launch-catastrophe-disaster/.

66 with the message "This link works": Joe Biden (@JoeBiden), "This link works," Twitter (now X), May 14, 2023, https://x.com/JoeBiden/status /1661496322980028423.

ENDNOTES

66 opposition to a "Don't Say Gay" bill: Andrew Atterbury, "DeSantis Revokes Disney's Special Status after 'Don't Say Gay' Opposition," *Politico*, April 22, 2022, https://www.politico.com/news/2022/04/22/desantis-disney-special-status-dont-say-gay-00027302.

67 "Man who called Biden 'Mr. Magoo' in Aug 2019": Twitter (now X), November 5, 2023, https://x.com/RonaldKlain/status/1721237196051460561?lang=en.

68 threatening to "destroy": Caleb Ecarma, "'I Will Destroy You': Biden Aide Threatened a *Politico* Reporter Pursuing a Story on His Relationship," *Vanity Fair*, February 12, 2021, https://www.vanityfair.com/news/2021/02/i-will-destroy-you-biden-aide-threatened-a-politico-reporter-pursuing-a-story-on-his-relationship?srsltid=AfmBOorY7cuZ2rUS6KA4DDIzU_WTRPCf_HuoOVMOE2jyB4B2IM6NQ_p.

68 "to deflect, to gaslight": Alexander Hall, "Axios Reporter Says White House Did 'Not Tell the Truth' for Years to Media, Themselves About Biden's Age," *Fox News*, June 28, 2024, https://www.foxnews.com/media/axios-reporter-says-white-house-did-not-tell-truth-years-media-themselves-about-bidens-age.

69 "We hope viewers enjoy watching what they tuned in for": Michael M. Grynbaum, "Biden to Sit Out Super Bowl Interview for Second Year in a Row," *New York Times*, February 3, 2024, https://www.nytimes.com/2024/02/03/business/media/biden-super-bowl-interview.html.

69 "well-meaning, elderly man": Jeannie Suk Gersen, "Why Robert Hur Called Biden an 'Elderly Man with a Poor Memory,'" *New Yorker*, March 22, 2024, https://www.newyorker.com/news/daily-comment/the-impossible-role-of-robert-hur.

72 Ukrainian "black ledger": Jack Gillum, Chad Day, and Jeff Horwitz, "Manafort Firm Received Ukraine Ledger Payout," Associated Press, April 12, 2017, https://apnews.com/article/20cfc75c82eb4a67b94e624e97207e23.

72 "They thought they snookered us": Paul Manafort, interview with author, May 16, 2024.

73 "pulling out of Trump Tower": Paul Manafort, interview with author, April 9, 2024.

74 "The guy is a thug": Paul Manafort, text to author, August 31, 2024.

74 "He *begged* Trump to let him come back": Paul Manafort, interview with author, August 16, 2024.

74 "Why would I beg": Corey Lewandowski, interview with author, September 24, 2024.

75 "no one's ever accused Corey Lewandowski of stealing a dime": Ibid.

75 "if you spend the money": Ibid.

75 LaCivita had been paid at least $22 million: Michael Isikoff, "Trump in Cash Crisis—As Campaign Chief's LLC's $19.2m Pay Revealed," *Daily Beast*, October 15, 2024, https://www.thedailybeast.com/donald-trumps-campaign-manager-chris-lacivitas-llc-multi-million-payday-revealed/.

75 "if you win, nobody cares": Corey Lewandowski, interview with author, September 24, 2024.

76 "Netflix-like mobile streaming": Isaac Stanley-Becker, Beth Reinhard, and Josh Dawsey, "Paul Manafort, Poised to Rejoin Trump World, Aided Chinese Media Deal," *Washington Post*, May 10, 2024, https://www.washingtonpost.com/politics/2024/05/10/paul-manafort-pardon-donald-trump-china/.

76 "a total bogus thing": Paul Manafort, interview with author, May 16, 2024.

77 "he's got a whole team now": Paul Manafort, interview with author, April 9, 2024.

77 "It could kill a small animal": Jazmine Ulloa and Alyce McFadden, "Trump Wants to Distance Himself From Project 2025. Democrats Are Trying Not to Let Him," *New York Times*, August 21, 2024, https://www.nytimes.com/2024/08/21/us/politics/project-2025-kenan-thompson.html.

77 "I have no idea who is behind it": Charles Homans, "A Project 2025 Leader Is Back in the Fold," *New York Times*, November 13, 2024, https://www.nytimes.com/2024/11/13/us/politics/project-2025-trump-heritage-foundation.html.

77 "They're doing the work now": Paul Manafort, interview with author, April 9, 2024.

78 *They exchanged glances*: Tim Alberta, "Trump Is Planning for a Landslide Win," *Atlantic*, July 10, 2024, https://www.theatlantic.com/politics/archive/2024/07/trump-campaign-election-2024-susie-wiles-chris-lacivita/678806/.

79 "This is crazy": Bill Daley, interview with author, August 12, 2024.

79 "I got rattled": Ibid.

79 "They were so cocky": Ibid.

80 "Do not do this": Ibid.

80 "one of the last people left in politics": Ezra Klein, "Nancy Pelosi: 'It Didn't Sound Like Joe Biden to Me,'" *New York Times*, August 9, 2024, https://www.nytimes.com/2024/08/09/opinion/ezra-klein-podcast-nancy-pelosi.html.

81 "Her accomplishments are overwhelming": Joe Biden, Remarks at Presentation of the Presidential Medal of Freedom, East Room of the White House, May 3, 2024, https://www.whitehouse.gov/briefing-room/speeches-remarks/2024/05/03/remarks-by-president-biden-at-presentation-of-the-presidential-medal-of-freedom-2/.

CHAPTER 5: "WE HAD A LONG TALK ABOUT AMERICA."

84 "what a great coach he is": Bruce Reed, interview with author, October 24, 2024.

84 "We sat around the table": Ron Klain, interview with author, September 8, 2024.

85 "the head of NATO": Ibid.

ENDNOTES

85 "super-triple-type A": Peter Baker, "A Hollywood Heavyweight Is Biden's Secret Weapon Against Trump," *New York Times*, June 13, 2024, https://www.nytimes.com/2024/06/13/us/politics/biden-jeffrey-katzenberg-trump.html.

85 "his infrastructure plan": Ron Klain, interview with author, September 8, 2024.

87 "on the core issues": Paul Manafort, interview with author, May 16, 2024.

88 "his voice had almost disappeared": Bruce Reed, interview with author, October 24, 2024.

88 "He's dead": Jonathan Martin, "'The Black Swan Election': Trump's Chiefs Tell Their Inside Story," December 19, 2024, https://www.politico.com/news/magazine/2024/12/19/trump-campaign-lacivita-fabrizio-qa-00195206.

88 "he wasn't dialed in": Ron Klain, interview with author, September 8, 2024.

88 "the most important thing is to keep talking": Bruce Reed, interview with author, October 24, 2024.

89 At a "debate watch party": Peter Baker, "A Fumbling Performance, and a Panicking Party," *New York Times*, June 27, 2024, https://www.nytimes.com/2024/06/27/us/politics/biden-debate-democrats.html.

89 "It's over": Gregory Krieg, MJ Lee, Jeff Zeleny, Arlette Saenz, Betsy Klein, and Camila DeChalus, "Donors Stress over Path Forward After Biden's Debate Performance," CNN, June 29, 2024, https://www.cnn.com/2024/06/29/politics/democratic-donors-biden-debate-election/index.html.

90 "They hated Donald Trump": Ryan Lizza, "Why Biden Was Really Forced Out of the Race, According to Anita Dunn," *Politico Magazine*, August 9, 2024, https://www.politico.com/news/magazine/2024/08/09/anita-dunn-no-regrets-biden-trump-debate-00173348.

91 "Just take a breath": Jeff Zients, interview with author, October 24, 2024.

91 "I know I'm not a young man": Joe Biden, Remarks at a Campaign Event, Raleigh, North Carolina, June 28, 2024, https://www.whitehouse.gov/briefing-room/speeches-remarks/2024/06/28/remarks-by-president-biden-at-a-campaign-event-raleigh-nc/.

91 "had chosen a risky presidential strategy": Ron Klain, interview with author, September 8, 2024.

92 "Look, we're hemorrhaging badly": Ibid.

92 "we've got a plan": Ibid.

93 "All you guys want to talk about": Ibid.

93 "Hey, what the fuck happened": Ibid.

94 "I believe in having people do their jobs": Ibid.

94 "I had hoped that the debate would provide some momentum": Catie Edmondson, "As Democratic Anxiety Rises, Doggett Calls on Biden

to Withdraw," *New York Times*, July 2, 2024, https://www.nytimes.com/2024/07/02/us/politics/lloyd-doggett-biden-withdraw.html.

95 "that's what this is about": "Full Transcript of ABC News' George Stephanopoulos' Interview with President Joe Biden," *ABC News*, August 19, 2021, https://abcnews.go.com/Politics/full-transcript-abc-news-george-stephanopoulos-interview-president/story?id=79535643.

95 "Heartbreaking": George Stephanopoulos, in an email to author, July 9, 2024.

95 "I'll bet you a million dollars": Ted Kaufman, interview with author, August 16, 2024.

95 "Pod Save Bros": Hugh Hewitt, "Opinion: Thank you, 'Pod Save America.' Really," *Washington Post*, September 16, 2024, https://www.washingtonpost.com/opinions/2024/09/16/pod-save-america-political-podcasts/.

95 "a cerebral, cool-guy president": Katie Rogers, "Pelosi and Others Try a New Tack with Biden: Is That Your Final Answer?," *New York Times*, July 10, 2024, https://www.nytimes.com/2024/07/10/us/politics/pelosi-biden-democrats.html.

95 "Joe Biden has been an extraordinary president": Jon Lovett (@jonlovett), X, July 10, 2024, https://x.com/jonlovett/status/1811086031531495457?lang=en.

96 "I am firmly committed to staying in this race": "Read the Letter President Biden Sent to House Democrats Telling Them to Support Him in the Election," Associated Press July 8, 2024, https://apnews.com/article/biden-letter-democrats-4562a72aa3a891e55261617d0d494d00.

96 "It didn't sound like Joe Biden to me": Ezra Klein, "Nancy Pelosi: 'It Didn't Sound Like Joe Biden to Me,'" *New York Times*, August 9, 2024, https://www.nytimes.com/2024/08/09/opinion/ezra-klein-podcast-nancy-pelosi.html.

96 *Anger has not worked*: Rogers, "Pelosi and Others Try a New Tack with Biden."

99 "I love Joe Biden": George Clooney, "I Love Joe Biden. But We Need a New Nominee," *New York Times*, July 10, 2024, https://www.nytimes.com/2024/07/10/opinion/joe-biden-democratic-nominee.html.

99 "I don't care, George": Ted Kaufman, interview with author, August 16, 2024.

100 "He wouldn't put a red light up": Bill Daley, interview with author, August 12, 2024.

103 "too delicious": Paul Manafort, text to author, July 11, 2024.

CHAPTER 6: "BLOOD ON EVERYONE IS JUST A MASSACRE."

105 "Let's move!": Amarachi Orie, Chris Liakos, and Andrew Millman, "What Was Said On Stage in the Seconds After Trump Was Shot," CNN, July 14, 2024, https://www.cnn.com/2024/07/14/politics/what-was-said-on-stage-after-trump-was-shot/index.html.

ENDNOTES

106 "a perfect storm of stunning failure": Richard Blumenthal (@SenBlumenthal), "What happened on July 13 was an accumulation of errors that produced a perfect storm of stunning failure. It was a tragedy & completely preventable from the outset," X, September 25, 2024, https://x.com/SenBlumenthal/status/1838947831794499900.

107 "now, tomorrow, and forever": Roy Reed, "Wallace, at Inauguration, Hints a New Race in 1972," *New York Times*, January 19, 1971, https://www.nytimes.com/1971/01/19/archives/wallace-at-inauguration-hints-a-new-race-in-1972.html.

107 "called for unity in the country": Brett Baier, *Fox News*, July 14, 2024.

107 "Let us reunite": CNN Staff, "Read the letter from Melania Trump responding to attempted assassination of Donald Trump," *CNN Politics*, July 14, 2024, https://www.cnn.com/2024/07/14/politics/melania-trump-statement-after-rally-shooting/index.html.

107 "I'm not supposed to be here": Michael Goodwin, "Grateful, Defiant Trump Recounts Surviving 'Surreal' Assassination Attempt at Rally: 'I'm Supposed to Be Dead,'" *New York Post*, July 14, 2024, https://nypost.com/2024/07/14/us-news/grateful-defiant-trump-recounts-surreal-assassination-attempt-at-rally-im-supposed-to-be-dead/.

108 "as if some ancient prophecy had been fulfilled": Anthony Lane, "The Republican National Convention and the Iconography of Triumph," *New Yorker*, July 25, 2024, https://www.newyorker.com/magazine/2024/08/05/the-republican-national-convention-and-the-iconography-of-triumph.

109 called him "America's Hitler": Mia McCarthy, "'I'm a Never Trump Guy': All of J.D. Vance's Trump Quotes That Could Come Back to Bite Him," *Politico*, July 15, 2024, https://www.politico.com/news/2024/07/15/jd-vance-donald-trump-comments-00168450.

109 "cultural heroin": Amy B. Wang and Meryl Kornfield, "The Not-So-Kind Things J.D. Vance Said About Trump Before He Was VP Pick," *Washington Post*, July 15, 2024, https://www.washingtonpost.com/elections/2024/07/15/jd-vance-trump-criticism/.

112 "I saw him get off the plane": Peter Baker, interview with author, September 3, 2024.

113 "We are prepped": Paul Manafort, text to author, July 18, 2024.

114 "That's my intention": Katie Rogers, Michael D. Shear, Peter Baker, and Zolan Kanno-Youngs, "Inside the Weekend When Biden Decided to Withdraw," *New York Times*, July 21, 2024, https://www.nytimes.com/2024/07/21/us/politics/biden-withdrawal-timeline.html.

114 "There's a path for you to win": White House email to the author, September 6, 2024.

115 "what would it look like": Ibid.

116 "I've decided not to run": Jeff Zients, interview with author, October 24, 2024.

119 "He's not running": Ron Klain, interview with author, September 8, 2024.

120 "a very bloody fight": Ibid.
122 "process": Evan Osnos, "Kamala Harris's Hundred-Day Campaign," *New Yorker*, October 13, 2024, https://www.newyorker.com/magazine /2024/10/21/kamala-harris-ascent.
122 "feeling isolated": Ron Klain, interview with author, September 8, 2024.
124 "#WinWithBlackWomen": Hannah Dormido, Eric Lau, Chris Alcantara, and Kati Perry, "Pro-Harris Groups Embrace Identity to Fundraise via Zoom," *Washington Post*, August 17, 2024, https://www.washingtonpost.com/elec tions/interactive/2024/zoom-calls-kamala-harris/.
124 "have to win *three* times?": Paul Manafort, interview with author, July 24, 2024.
126 "Happy Warrior": Melissa Quinn, Nikole Killion, and Fin Gómez, "Obama Endorses Harris for President, Solidifying Democratic Support," CBS News, July 26, 2024, https://www.cbsnews.com/news/obama-en dorses-kamala-harris-president-2024-election/.
126 warning of the "Harris honeymoon": Isaac Schorr, "Trump's Long-time Pollster Predicts Kamala Harris 'Honeymoon' Will See Her Gain on and Even Beat Him in Polls," msn.com, July 23, 2024, https://www .msn.com/en-us/news/politics/trump-s-longtime-pollster-predicts-kamala -harris-honeymoon-will-see-her-gain-on-and-even-beat-him-in-polls/ar -BB1qv7tX?ocid=BingNewsVerp.

CHAPTER 7: "THIS COUNTRY IS NOTHING LIKE IT WAS IN 1968."

128 "pounded and clubbed and gassed and beaten": Norman Mailer, *Miami and the Siege of Chicago* (New York: Random House, 1968).
129 "nothing like it was in 1968": Bill Daley, interview with author, August 12, 2024.
129 "good crowds": Ibid.
131 "Teddy's out": Ibid.
132 "swelling energy and excitement": Robert Draper, "Joe Biden's Interrupted Presidency," *New York Times Magazine*, August 18, 2024, https://www.ny times.com/2024/08/18/magazine/joe-biden-president-legacy.html.
136 *Not a good night*: Paul Manafort, text to author, August 20, 2024.
137 "I didn't know she was Black": Lisa Lerer and Maya King, "Trump Re-marks on Harris Evoke a Haunting and Unsettling History," *New York Times*, July 31, 2024, https://www.nytimes.com/2024/07/31/us/politics /trump-harris-race.html.
137 "dumber than hell": Brett Samuels, "Trump Doubles Down on Insults and Mockery in Attacks on Harris," *The Hill*, October 13, 2024, https://thehill .com/homenews/campaign/4929331-trump-insults-harris/.
137 "lazy": Thomas Beaumont and Jill Colvin, "Trump Hurls a String of In-sults at Harris, including 'Lazy,' a Racist Trope against Black People," AP, October 23, 2024, https://apnews.com/article/trump-kamala-lazy-trope -stereotype-4c2ded1046e492c5d24c7382245d0f7b.

137 "blow jobs impacted both their careers": Michael Gold, "Trump Reposts Crude Sexual Remark About Harris on Truth Social," *New York Times*, August 28, 2024, https://www.nytimes.com/2024/08/28/us/politics/trump-truth-social-posts.html.

137 "like she's a worthy opponent": Kellyanne Conway, interview with author, September 18, 2024.

138 "President Trump is for you": Shane Goldmacher, "Trump and Republicans Bet Big on Anti-Trans Ads Across the Country," *New York Times*, October 8, 2024, https://www.nytimes.com/2024/10/08/us/politics/trump-republican-transgender-ads.html.

139 "blue wall": Kinsey Crowley, "What Is the 'Blue Wall'? Latest Polls from Key States of Michigan, Pennsylvania, Wisconsin," *USA Today*, October 29, 2024, https://www.usatoday.com/story/news/politics/elections/2024/10/29/blue-wall-states/75912615007/.

140 "Scranton Joe": Amie Parnes and Morgan Chalfant, "Why Pennsylvania Is So Personally, Politically Important to 'Scranton Joe,'" *The Hill*, September 4, 2022, https://thehill.com/homenews/administration/3626443-why-pennsylvania-is-so-personally-politically-important-to-scranton-joe/.

140 "childless cat ladies": Aaron Blake, "The Trump Campaign Can't Quit 'Childless Cat Ladies,'" *Washington Post*, September 18, 2024, https://www.washingtonpost.com/politics/2024/09/18/trump-sanders-harris-childless-cat-ladies/.

140 "That's my dad!": Jonathan J. Cooper, "'That's My Dad!': Gus Walz Tearfully Cheers on His Father as He Accepts Democratic VP Nomination," Associated Press, August 22, 2024, https://apnews.com/article/gus-walz-thats-my-dad-dnc-523c5add372384a810af9e8501dc07ba.

CHAPTER 8: "THEY'RE EATING THE DOGS, THEY'RE EATING THE CATS."

145 21.797 million viewers: Mark Mwachiro, "Here Are the Final Ratings for 2024 Convention Coverage," *Adweek*, August 26, 2024, https://www.adweek.com/tvnewser/2024-dnc-rnc-final-ratings/.

145 "race to lose": Eli Yokley and Cameron Easley, "No Convention Bump for Harris, Who Nonetheless Remains in the Driver's Seat," *Morning Consult*, August 26, 2024, https://pro.morningconsult.com/analysis/kamala-harris-dnc-polling.

145 *"That is called Bidenomics"*: Daily Wire News, "Trump Campaign Releases Ad Targeting Harris Over Inflation, Americans Struggling to Make Ends Meet," *Daily Wire*, August 17, 2024, https://www.dailywire.com/news/trump-campaign-releases-ad-targeting-harris-over-inflation-americans-struggling-to-make-ends-meet.

146 "border czar": Cecelia Smith-Schoenwalder, "New Trump Ad Targets Harris on Immigration, Calls Her a Failed 'Border Czar,'" *US News & World Report*, July 30, 2024, https://www.usnews.com/news/national

-news/articles/2024-07-30/trump-ad-targets-harris-on-immigration-calls
-her-a-failed-border-czar.

146 "northern triangle": Zolan Kanno-Youngs and Jazmine Ulloa, "As Republicans Attack Harris on Immigration, Here's What Her Record Shows,"
New York Times, July 31, 2024, https://www.nytimes.com/2024/07/31/us
/politics/kamala-harris-immigration.html.

146 "amnesty": Daniel Dale, "Fact Check: New Trump Ad Uses Edited Quote
to Attack Nonexistent Harris Immigration Proposal," CNN, August 31,
2024, https://www.cnn.com/2024/08/31/politics/fact-check-trump-ad-har
ris-immigration/index.html.

146 "We're not going back!": Jeff Stein, Yasmeen Abutaleb, and Dan Dia-
mond, "Kamala Harris Unveils Populist Policy Agenda, with $6,000
Credit for Newborns," *Washington Post*, August 16, 2024, https://www
.washingtonpost.com/business/2024/08/16/kamala-harris-2024-policy
-child-tax-credit/.

147 "sex change": Donald Trump (@realdonaldtrump), Instagram, October 20,
2024, https://www.instagram.com/realdonaldtrump/reel/DBWLiw9Odb6
/?hl=en.

147 "Swift Boat Veterans for Truth": Jodi Wilgoren, "Vietnam Veterans Buy
Ads to Attack Kerry," *New York Times*, August 5, 2004, https://www
.nytimes.com/2004/08/05/us/vietnam-veterans-buy-ads-to-attack-kerry
.html.

147 "Try and top that": Adam Nagourney and Nicholas Nehamas, "Harris Loss Has Democrats Fighting Over How to Talk About Transgender Rights," *New York Times*, November 20, 2024, https://www.nytimes
.com/2024/11/20/us/politics/presidential-campaign-transgender-rights
.html.

149 "policy time": Jonathan Swan, Maggie Haberman, Katie Rogers, and
Reid J. Epstein, "Inside the Trump-Harris Debate Prep: Method Acting,
Insults, Tough Questions," *New York Times*, September 7, 2024, https://
www.nytimes.com/2024/09/07/us/politics/trump-harris-debate-prep
.html.

149 "he's moved on": Paul Manafort, interview with author, September 10,
2024.

149 leading Harris by 48 to 47 percent: Mia McCarthy, "Harris, Trump
Deadlocked in New *New York Times* Poll," *Politico*, September 8, 2024,
https://www.politico.com/news/2024/09/08/harris-trump-latest-poll-001
77875.

149 "WHEN I WIN": Josh Fiallo, "Donald Trump Already Casting Doubt
Over Election Results in Truth Social Rant," *Daily Beast*, September 17,
2024, https://www.thedailybeast.com/donald-trump-already-casting-doubt
-over-prez-election-results-in-truth-social-rant/.

149 "Weekends are always tough": Paul Manafort, interview with author,
September 10, 2024.

150 "Very Online influencers": Tim Alberta, "Inside the Ruthless, Restless Fi-

nal Days of Trump's Campaign," *Atlantic*, November 2, 2024, https://www.theatlantic.com/politics/archive/2024/11/trump-2024-campaign-lewandowski-conway/680456/.

150 "pets abducted and eaten": Ibid.
151 Oxford debate: "Oxford Style Debate," United States Courts, https://www.uscourts.gov/about-federal-courts/educational-resources/about-educational-outreach/activity-resources/oxford.
151 "as staggering as it was indisputable": John Heilemann, "Slaughterhouse Five," *Puck*, September 15, 2024, https://puck.news/a-post-debate-meltdown-is-consuming-trumpworld/.
152 "He actually won the Haitian thing": Brad Parscale, interview with author, September 18, 2024.
153 childless cat lady: Taylor Swift (taylorswift), Instagram, September 20, 2024, https://www.instagram.com/taylorswift/p/C_wtAOKOW1z/?hl=en.
153 a "cancer": Ken Bensinger, "Laura Loomer, a Social-Media Instigator, Is Back at Trump's Side," *New York Times*, September 12, 2024, https://www.nytimes.com/2024/09/12/us/politics/trump-laura-loomer.html.
155 "change candidate": Shane Goldmacher, "Who's the Change Candidate?," *New York Times*, August 21, 2024, https://www.nytimes.com/2024/08/21/briefing/harris-trump-2024-election-change.html.
156 "A flood of illegals": Maggie Haberman, "In Trump Ad, 'Not a Thing Comes to Mind' Ties Harris to Biden's Liabilities," *New York Times*, October 21, 2024, https://www.nytimes.com/2024/10/21/us/politics/trump-ad-harris-biden.html.
156 $853 million: Shane Goldmacher and Maggie Haberman, "Kamala Harris Has Raised $1 Billion Since Entering 2024 Presidential Race," *New York Times*, October 9, 2024, https://www.nytimes.com/2024/10/09/us/politics/harris-billion-dollar-fundraising.html.
157 14.5 million followers: Michael Gold and Reid J. Epstein, "Trump to Go on Joe Rogan's Podcast, a Play to Reach Less Likely Voters," *New York Times*, October 22, 2024, https://www.nytimes.com/2024/10/22/us/politics/trump-joe-rogan-podcast.html.
157 thirty-two false claims: Daniel Dale, "Fact Check: 32 False Claims Trump Made to Joe Rogan," CNN, October 27, 2024, https://www.cnn.com/2024/10/27/politics/fact-check-trump-rogan-podcast/index.html.
157 "pulled around on a nose-ring": David Zimmermann, "J.D. Vance to appear on Rogan Podcast after Host Rejects Kamala Interview over Campaign Demands," *National Review*, October 29, 2024, https://www.nationalreview.com/news/joe-rogan-rejected-kamala-harris-interview-over-campaign-demands/.
157 Word of this dissension: Joshua Franklin and Anna Nicolaou, "Kamala Harris Ditched Joe Rogan Podcast Interview over Progressive Backlash Fears," *Financial Times*, November 14, 2024, https://www.ft.com/content/9292db59-8291-4507-8d86-f8d4788da467.
157 "VP didn't appear on Rogan because of schedule," Jennifer Palmieri

(@jmpalmieri), X, November 3, 2024, https://x.com/jmpalmieri/status/1856807303171002554.

158 "Trump amnesia": Susan Glasser, "Donald Trump's Amnesia Advantage," *New Yorker*, April 4, 2024, https://www.newyorker.com/news/letter-from-bidens-washington/donald-trumps-amnesia-advantage.

158 "filled with losers": Jeffrey Goldberg, "Trump: Americans Who Died in War Are 'Losers' and 'Suckers,'" *Atlantic*, September 3, 2020, https://www.theatlantic.com/politics/archive/2020/09/trump-americans-who-died-at-war-are-losers-and-suckers/615997/.

159 "he's certainly an authoritarian": Michael S. Schmidt, "As Election Nears, Kelly Warns Trump Would Rule Like a Dictator," *New York Times*, October 22, 2024, https://www.nytimes.com/2024/10/22/us/politics/john-kelly-trump-fitness-character.html.

CHAPTER 9: "AN ISLAND OF GARBAGE"

161 "Pro-American Rally": Sarah Kate Kramer, "When Nazis Took Manhattan," NPR, February 20, 2019, https://www.npr.org/sections/codeswitch/2019/02/20/695941323/when-nazis-took-manhattan.

162 wished "his generals": Jeffrey Goldberg, "'I Need the Kind of Generals That Hitler Had,'" *Atlantic*, October 22, 2024, https://www.theatlantic.com/politics/archive/2024/10/trump-military-generals-hitler/680327/.

163 "Tampon Tim": Rachel Treisman, "Why Republicans Are Calling Walz 'Tampon Tim'—and Why Democrats Embrace It," NPR, August 7, 2024, https://www.npr.org/2024/08/07/nx-s1-5066878/tim-walz-tampon-law-minnesota.

163 "the closing argument": Stephen Collinson, "Trump Unveils the Most Extreme Closing Argument in Modern Presidential History," CNN, October 28, 2024, https://www.cnn.com/2024/10/28/politics/trump-extreme-closing-argument/index.html.

164 "shall be returned to the American people": History.com Editors, "This Day in History, 1939: Americans Hold a Nazi Rally in Madison Square Garden," *History.com*, https://www.history.com/this-day-in-history/americans-hold-nazi-rally-in-madison-square-garden.

164 "America First": Cyrus Veeser, "History Shows How Dangerous 'America First' Really Is," *Time*, September 10, 2024, https://time.com/7006686/history-america-first-dawes/.

164 interview with Trump: Maggie Haberman and David E. Sanger, "Transcript: Donald Trump Expounds on His Foreign Policy Views," *New York Times*, March 27, 2016, https://www.nytimes.com/2016/03/27/us/politics/donald-trump-transcript.html.

165 "the nastier the nickname": Susan B. Glasser, "Garbage Time at the 2024 Finish Line," *New Yorker*, October 31, 2024, https://www.newyorker.com/news/letter-from-bidens-washington/garbage-time-at-the-2024-finish-line.

ENDNOTES

165 "America's mayor": Azi Paybarah, "How Giuliani Went From America's Mayor to Trump's Lawyer," *New York Times*, December 10, 2019, https://www.nytimes.com/2019/12/10/nyregion/rudy-giuliani-nyc.html.

167 call the event a "lovefest": Brett Samuels, "Trump Calls Madison Square Garden Rally a 'Love Fest,'" *Daily Beast*, October 29, 2024, https://thehill.com/homenews/4959432-trump-ny-msg-rally-love-fest/.

167 "fans the fuel of hate": Nikki Carvajal, "Harris Says Trump 'Fans the Fuel of Hate and Division' After Madison Square Garden Rally," CNN, October 28, 2024, https://www.cnn.com/2024/10/28/politics/harris-reaction-trump-madison-square-garden-rally/index.html.

167 "No one wakes up": Jennifer Ridder, interview with author, November 17, 2024.

169 "hateful rhetoric": Zolan Kanno-Youngs, "Biden Appears to Insult Trump Supporters as 'Garbage,' but Quickly Tries to Clarify," *New York Times*, October 29, 2024, https://www.nytimes.com/2024/10/29/us/politics/biden-garbage-trump-supporters.html.

169 "deplorables": Jonathan Swan and Maggie Haberman, "Trump and His Allies Link Biden's 'Garbage' Comment to 2016 'Deplorables' Remark," *New York Times*, October 29, 2024, https://www.nytimes.com/2024/10/29/us/politics/biden-trump-supporters-garbage-reaction.html.

170 "the most evil mass murderers in history": Brooke Singman, "'Treated You Like Garbage': Trump Uses Biden Criticism as Rallying Cry in Battleground North Carolina," *Fox News*, October 30, 2024, https://www.foxnews.com/politics/treated-you-like-garbage-trump-uses-biden-criticism-rallying-cry-battleground-north-carolina.

170 "We're winning and her vote is underperforming": Paul Manafort, interview with author, October 31, 2024.

172 "Teflon president": Joanna Weiss, "Pat Schroeder Mastered Using Humor in Politics, Long Before Social Media," *Politico Magazine*, March 17, 2023, https://www.politico.com/news/magazine/2023/03/17/pat-schroeder-remembrance-00087429.

172 "win the country": Shane Goldmacher and Ken Bensinger, "Republicans Built an Ecosystem of Influencers. Some Democrats Want One, Too," *New York Times*, November 28, 2024, https://www.nytimes.com/2024/11/28/us/politics/democratic-influencers.html.

172 "well-oiled": David Plouffe, "The Harris Campaign on What Went Wrong," *Pod Save America*, November 26, 2024, https://crooked.com/podcast/exclusive-the-harris-campaign-on-what-went-wrong/.

173 "time for Trump to hang up his hat": Elon Musk (@elonmusk), "I don't hate the man, but it's time for Trump to hang up his hat & sail into the sunset. Dems should also call off the attack—don't make it so that Trump's only way to survive is to regain the Presidency," Twitter (now X), July 11, 2022, https://x.com/elonmusk/status/1546669610509799424.

173 "clown, genius, edgelord": Molly Ball, Jeffrey Kluger, and Alejandro de la

Garza, "Time 2021 Person of the Year: Elon Musk," *Time*, December 13, 2021, https://time.com/person-of-the-year-2021-elon-musk/.

174 would be "fucked" if: Miles Klee and Asawin Suebsaeng, "Republicans Were Ready to Torch Elon Musk for Blowing the Election. Then Trump Won," *Rolling Stone*, November 20, 2024, https://www.rollingstone.com /politics/politics-features/trump-musk-republicans-stuck-election-2024-1 235173757/.

174 "wants to take away your freedom of speech": Ryan Mac, "Elon Musk Leaps to Trump's Side in Rally Appearance," *New York Times*, October 5, 2024, https://www.nytimes.com/2024/10/05/us/politics/elon -musk-trump-butler-rally.html.

175 "very strange man": Klee and Suebsaeng, "Republicans Were Ready to Torch Elon Musk."

175 "the Trump team is on its back foot": Harris for President/Democratic National Committee Campaign Memos, Democracy in Action, September 1, 2024, https://www.democracyinaction.us/2024/candidates/harris memos.html.

176 "the race has changed": Paul Manafort, interview with author, August 16, 2024.

CHAPTER 10: "YOU CAN'T TALK PEOPLE OUT OF THAT FEELING."

177 "shouldn't have left": Michael Gold, Maggie Haberman, and Shane Goldmacher, "Trump, in Increasingly Dark and Dour Tones, Says He 'Shouldn't Have Left' the White House," *New York Times*, November 3, 2024, https://www.nytimes.com/2024/11/03/us/politics/trump-pa-rally-election .html.

184 "consistent polling results": Jennifer Ridder, interview with author, November 17, 2024.

185 Harris would win Iowa by three points: Brianne Pfannenstiel, "Iowa Poll. Kamala Harris leapfrogs Donald Trump to take lead near Election Day. Here's how," *Des Moines Register*, November 2, 2024, https:// www.desmoinesregister.com/story/news/politics/iowa-poll/2024/11/02 /iowa-poll-kamala-harris-leads-donald-trump-2024-presidential-race /75354033007/.

185 "You get sucked into the momentum": Lorraine Voles, interview with author, December 9, 2024.

186 "We went and sat in my car": Ibid.

186 "public reporting was not that optimistic": Ron Klain, interview with author, November 9, 2024.

187 "Trump is going to win": Ibid.

190 "a nearly flawless campaign": Jess Bidgood and Shane Goldmacher, "Fighting Over a 'Flawless' Campaign," *New York Times*, December 6, 2024, https://www.nytimes.com/2024/12/06/us/politics/trump-harris-cam paign-meeting.html.

ENDNOTES

190 40 out of 54 incumbent parties were defeated: David Rising, Jill Lawless, and Nicholas Riccardi, "The 'super year' of elections has been super bad for incumbents as voters punish them in droves," AP, November 17, 2024, https://apnews.com/article/global-elections-2024-incumbents-defeated-c80fbd4e667de86fe08aac025b333f95#.

191 "With the 'save democracy people'": Paul Manafort, interview with author, November 27, 2024.

EPILOUGE: "IT DIDN'T SEEM LIKE SHE EVEN TRIED"

196 Manafort had been pitching his services: Kenneth P. Vogel, Kim Barker, Constant Méheut, and Michael Schwirtz, "Pardoned by Trump, Manafort Is Back and Looking for Foreign Work," *New York Times*, January 12, 2025, https://www.nytimes.com/2025/01/12/us/politics/trump-manafort.html.

200 "the luster seemed to come off her": Susie Wiles, interview with author, January 11, 2025.

203 "we now bear the fruit of that failed leadership": Leon Panetta, interview with author, January 16, 2025.

ABOUT THE AUTHOR

CHRIS WHIPPLE is a *New York Times* bestselling author and widely acclaimed documentary filmmaker, speaker, as well as a Peabody and Emmy Award–winning journalist. He appears throughout the media and contributes to the *New York Times* and *Washington Post,* and has written for *Vanity Fair, Politico,* and the *Daily Beast,* among others. He lives in Clinton, Connecticut, with his wife, Cary.